the
SHEEPSKIN
PSYCHOSIS

By the Same Author:

THEY FOUGHT ALONE
THE INSOLENT CHARIOTS
SCHOOLS WITHOUT SCHOLARS
THE CRACK IN THE PICTURE WINDOW

the SHEEPSKIN PSYCHOSIS

by John Keats

PHILADELPHIA AND NEW YORK

J. B. LIPPINCOTT COMPANY

Foreword

Early in 1963, Life magazine asked me to write 6,000
words on college dropouts. After the article was fin-
ished, I somewhat morosely surveyed sixty-three pages
of notes acquired during the course of research and
realized that something else remained to be said.

Briefly, it seemed time to say that the idea of going
to college has been wildly oversold to the public.

I cannot believe that a college education would be
a good thing for everybody. I am convinced that too
many, not too few, high school graduates go to college. Instead of building community colleges, I think
we would do better to improve the content in our
high schools. Instead of seeking ways to admit more
students to our universities, I believe our universities
should become more selective.

It occurs to me that we all use terms like *youth,
college,* and *society* rather loosely. Unfortunately, we

can do little else here, because we are not dealing with something that you and I can pick up, inspect, and weigh like a grapefruit. Instead, we are dealing with the different, changing abilities and emotions of more than three million students, no two of them alike; with thousands of colleges of many different sorts that range from institutions less sophisticated and informative than many an urban high school to such great universities as those of the Ivy League. Nearly all of these colleges are in flux, and so are the students, and all this within a society that is rapidly changing and wildly multiplying without any clear sense of direction or discernible purpose. Indeed, if America can be said to have a national goal, it would seem merely a vague notion that everyone should make a little money and have a good time, with ends and means left up to the individual.

In this utter formlessness, it is just as risky for me to deal with specific matters as it is to compose generalities. But I see nothing for it but to do both, even though this means I am saddling you with the responsibility of deciding if the particular thing I mention is generally applicable to your experience, and whether the general statements I make can be applied to the particular circumstances in your neighborhood. The American experience is so variously hued that it well-nigh defies analysis. But defiance is always an invitation.

You may wish to know that the voices quoted herein are those of real people, tape-recorded in private homes, at employment offices, and on campuses in the East, Midwest, and Far West. The campuses were those of private colleges large and small; of teachers colleges, state universities, engineering colleges, and large city

6

universities that draw the bulk of their students from their cities. While I cannot pretend that this book is scholarly, or definitive, I do suggest it represents what might be called a fair national sample of attitudes and opinions. For reasons that seem sufficient to me, I have preserved the privacy of my informants. Robert E. Iffert is an exception to this rule because he is a senior official of the Department of Health, Education and Welfare's Office of Education, and is the author of the Government's standard work dealing with the reasons why students attend—and leave—college. He was interviewed, for publication, in his official capacity. I am much indebted to him for his time and his courtesy. Quotation from printed work is designated as such, and attribution is made.

You may assume that all opinions herein, not otherwise accredited to specific sources, are my own. This raises the question of my credentials as a critic of higher education. I have none, other than United States citizenship.

—John Keats

Contents

the
SHEEPSKIN
PSYCHOSIS

1

Somewhat oversold?

"Influential friends, religious conversions and intensive coaching on tests are the latest weapons in a strange new conflict—competition among 3-year-olds and 4-year-olds for admission to private nursery schools."

So Martin Tolchin reported in *The New York Times,* February 17, 1964. He quoted one mother as saying, " 'If you can get them in at 4, you can breathe until they're 18.' "

"To create a favorable impression during the interviews, mothers determine whether a nursery school is psyche-oriented, society-oriented, or intellect-oriented," Mr. Tolchin wrote. "This determines whether a child arrives at the school in overalls or short pants and knee-length socks.

"A mother now making the rounds asked:

" 'I wonder if it won't be held against me that my son doesn't have an English haircut. But I don't want him to look like a sheepdog.' "

In case you are wondering just who these people could possibly be, let me assure you that their name is legion. They are your neighbors and mine in almost any urban community east of the Mississippi, but their activity is most highly visible in New York City, where applications outnumber vacancies by as much as 150 to 1 at some of the city's 400 private nursery schools.

The scramble for admission is not pretty. At least 2 out of every 100 applicants show evidence that they have been coached on the Stanford-Binet standard intelligence tests by ambitious parents, Mr. Tolchin reported. He said parents would change their religions to ensure their children's acceptance at church-affiliated nursery schools, often becoming converts before their children could walk, and working hard at volunteer activities to ingratiate themselves with the congregations.

"Nursery schools affiliated with elementary and high schools are much sought after because they allow a 13-year respite from the academic steeplechase," Mr. Tolchin wrote. "Once in such a nursery school, a child's next problem is getting into college."

Not all communities suffer from a mood as intense as New York City's, but the differences are of detail, not of kind. Parents have considerable reason to believe that a child will not get into a good college unless he has a good preparation. While elsewhere parents may act on this belief by moving into a public school district noted for its excellence, or by sending their children to private high schools, the circumstances in New York are such that parents believe—not without reason—that if a child does not go to a good nursery school, he cannot get into a good *grade school*, then

14

not into a good high school that will prepare him for the good college.

Perhaps the most remarkable aspect of the parental anxiety is that it is not primarily concerned with education.

It is concerned with jobs.

The national preoccupation with college admission is rooted in the belief that a young man cannot hope to find a good job today unless he has a college diploma. There is abundant evidence to support this belief, and we shall discuss that evidence in due course. At this point, however, it is relevant to state that widespread insistence on a diploma, as an indispensable condition of employment, is a fairly recent development in American life. There was nothing like it before the Second World War. It seems to have begun its epidemic growth shortly after that war, with Federal assistance. It was then that the Labor Department first published the statistical fact that, on average, a college graduate would earn $100,000 more during his lifetime than a man who had only a high school diploma would earn. At the same time, the Federal Government subsidized the college educations of returned veterans. In the years that followed, many interrelated factors worked to increase college enrollments. Continued prosperity played a part. So did the steady increase in population, the drift from rural areas to the cities, the increasing complexity in technical jobs, automation, the steady diminution of demand for hand-wrought products and for unskilled labor, growing acceptance of the financial theory that one can live comfortably on perpetually extended credit; so did fear of the draft. I do not pretend this list of factors is definitive. I merely wish to suggest that changing

15

circumstances of many sorts have conspired to make a college education more appealing and more available to a greater number of high school graduates than ever before in our history. The Federal Government meanwhile has continued to give its constant blessing to the notion that every high school graduate who can do college work should go to college.

During the postwar years, as a greater proportion of the nation's youth began to go to college, employers increasingly found themselves in a buyer's market. Matters have progressed to the point where one Ohio businessman can now say that he will hire no one but Ohio State University graduates to drive his trucks. It is not that he is convinced an Ohio State education is the nation's best course in driver training. He puts the matter on other grounds:

"If a kid shows me an OSU diploma, that tells me he's spent four years plugging away at *something*," the businessman said. "He's serious. I don't expect him to be a truck driver all his life. But if he's spent four years at one thing, the chances are that he'll stick with me for a while, and while he does, the chances are that he won't be a wise guy, or goof off, or hand in fake gas bills, or join the union."

To some people, the Ohio businessman's beliefs may seem as bizarre as his logic, but his practice is only slightly more peculiar than that of the corporation talent scouts who invade the campuses each spring to recruit employees for the junior management training programs. In nearly all these cases, the employers are looking for basic qualities, rather than for specific intellectual accomplishments. They say they are looking for clarity of mind; for people who can generalize from broad knowledge; for people with cultural back-

16

grounds. They are quite right in believing that such people arc more often found in colleges than anywhere else, although there is a considerable question as to whether these qualities are always put to use within our corporations. It is also debatable whether a college education actually increases one's clarity of thought, or ability to synthesize, and, as we shall see, there is reason to doubt that today's college education could be called broad, or concerned with cultural values.

But the talent scouts are not interested in such speculations. Nor do they dwell on the probability that many graduates will have sneaked through college on lesson-learning ability without ever asking a question or forming a synthesis. The scouts are simply fishing in a pool known in the past to contain large fish rather than trying their luck in unknown waters. The real point of the exercise is to simplify the job of the personnel manager, who considers his task more than half done if he can put the applications of college graduates into his In basket and toss those of the non-graduates into the wastebasket.

"I don't say this is right; I do say this is how it is," a Philadelphia banker said. "Suppose you had two boys applying for a job. Either of them could do the work, but one has a college diploma, and one has not. Which would *you* take? Say they both had diplomas, but one boy had gone to Harvard and the other had gone to some small Western school you never heard of. Which would *you* take?"

There is evidence that the banker's view is as widely condemned as it is widely shared—it is sometimes condemned even by those who share it. But no one seems willing to pioneer a different approach. Rather, employers tend to agree with the purchasing agent of one

17

giant corporation who said, "We hire no one but college graduates because we can always find enough of them."

This practice dismays Robert E. Iffert, a senior official of the Department of Health, Education and Welfare's Office of Education. Mr. Iffert is author of *Retention and Withdrawal of College Students*, a study of the hopes, motivations, and disappointments of college students.

"Society is unfair to itself," Mr. Iffert said. "Any industry, or employer, is unfair to himself for putting that much credence in the record."

Mr. Iffert said it was perfectly plain that many boys who never went to college could do as well in a given job as many college graduates, or better; that a boy who failed out of Princeton might well be a better candidate for an intellectually demanding task than the *cum laude* graduate of many another institution, or sometimes be a stronger candidate than a boy who was graduated from Princeton with honor.

The headmaster of one private preparatory school agreed. He added that employers might sometimes do themselves a great disservice by insisting on college graduates, because a diploma is not necessarily a guarantee of character or quality. Many college boys, he said, are nothing more than time-serving conformists.

On the other hand, it might be said that the only risk our corporations run in hiring college graduates is that some of the graduates will be too bright. It happens that a superior mind can be a real handicap, because the rule is that most employers will look askance at the young man who has done too well in college.

18

"If I have a choice between an A student from Massachusetts Institute of Technology and a B student from any other engineering school, I will take that B student every time," said the personnel director of a large industrial concern. "Why? Because the A student from M.I.T. is going to go off by himself in a corner somewhere. He'll want to fool around with theories. He'll want to do some Goddamned research that isn't worth a cent to anybody, but the B student is going to be practical. You tell him what you want done, and he'll sit down and do it for you."

"I can see the point," a stockbroker said. "I wouldn't want to hire the A student either, because he's not the employee type. He'll want to be the employer. He'll work for you just as long as it takes him to learn the business, and then he's gone to start in business for himself with some of your clients. The most valuable guy in our office is a real dumbbell. My God, he's dumb! It takes him longer to learn something than it takes anybody else, but once he's got it, he never makes a mistake, and you never have to worry about that part of the operation again. And the best thing about him is that he's so dumb he's happy to do what he's told."

"I suppose there is a place for brilliance," a Washington newspaper editor said. "But not on this newspaper. We need placid people for the long pull."

"The A student will be narrow, an introvert," a California real estate man said. "But the C student—and he may have got some Ds—will be broad and gregarious."

"We make no distinction between colleges," the hiring officer of one huge business firm said, in contradistinction to the Philadelphia banker. But then he added: "We treat equally the application of the boy from the Bob Jones University of Dayton, Tennessee, and that of the boy from Harvard—although, as a matter of fact, we prefer to recruit from the more obscure colleges, because we are looking for the more normal, average boy."

Asked to define the "normal, average boy," he eventually identified him as one of modest abilities and attainments. He said there was nothing in his firm's work that required the slightest academic training. Once the company hired a college graduate, it would then train him for the routine job he was to hold. Asked why the company insisted on hiring college graduates if it was looking for mediocrity to press into a mold, the hiring officer said nothing about the possible virtues of a college education, and nothing about the presumable character of a college man. He merely repeated what so many employers say: You can always find enough of them. Asked if he did not think his company's hiring practices might possibly be improved upon, he said, "No, why tamper with success? We have found that our way works well enough." Like Shakespeare's Caesar, he seemed to prefer about him fat, sleek-headed men, such as sleep o' nights.

Further examples could be cited, all serving the point that the standards of the academic world are different from those of the workaday world. What the one prizes, the other deplores. The public attitude is somewhat contradictory, for as parents, we want our children to go to the best colleges and earn high honors, while as employers, we are suspicious of brilliance and prefer mediocrity. We tend to regard the diploma as a kind of working paper, rather than as evidence of laudable attainments in the arts. We seem to be saying that we have no use for such laudable attainments, yet we increasingly insist that job applicants be at least bachelors of the arts, and this insistence has been carried to such extremes that the entire nation seems to suffer from what one exasperated parent called a sheepskin psychosis.

The national mood would certainly seem one of frantic anxiety, stemming from the fact that while most Americans believe every child should have an opportunity to go to college, they know very well that not every child can get in—including large numbers of students qualified for admission. A problem is that the postwar population increased at a faster rate than college facilities expanded. For example, the dean of admissions at one Midwestern state university said, "Even if we had started to build new facilities two years ago—which we didn't—we could not possibly accommodate the number of applicants we will have two years from now.

"There is no doubt that the children are going to come here," he said. "They are born, and they are going through high school today. They are going to come, and we will not be able to take care of them. We will not have the teachers, and we will not have the classrooms, and we will not have the dormitories."

The parental anxiety is compounded by the refusal of the most prestigious private colleges to increase greatly in size. This tightens the screw, because most Americans believe—with considerable practical justification—that the better the college, the better the student's chances in life, and that the highly selective Ivy League colleges are the best colleges of all. These schools now receive applications from six times as many well-qualified high school seniors as they can

21

accept—to the great despair of the five families whose sons are turned down for no reason other than lack of space. The result is that the Ivy League rejects spill over into the lesser private colleges, which happily raise their standards of admission to Ivy levels, thus squeezing out less-gifted applicants who might in other times have got into these schools. Whereupon there is another spillover into colleges of the third rank, and so on down the line. The pitiful end result is a desperate search on the part of parents of rather dull students for some kind of college that will accept their children. It is this last, desperate search that is responsible for the current popular interest in "junior colleges" and in the construction of "community colleges"— both euphemisms for postgraduate high school education of one sort or another. The idea here is that a boy simply must have a diploma from *somewhere* if he is to acquire a job; a diploma from *something* that can be called "college."

Perhaps at this point we should ask for a time-out, in order to determine just what kind of game we are playing; to find out what the rules are; to decide whether we really want to go on playing it. For example, sober reflection will disclose that we do not all agree on what there is about a job that makes it *good*. Nor do we agree on what a college education should be. For that matter, most adult Americans have no personal knowledge of what a college is, since most of us have never been to one. Nor do we always try to find out what connection there is between going to college and working at any of the thousands of jobs which demand none of the skills that can be acquired only in college.

It would help to clear the air if we immediately dis-

22

tinguished between the terms *education* and *training*. Both take place on a university campus. Education is concerned with concepts rather than with vocational techniques. It involves an ability to discriminate; it has to do with learning to learn, and at least one of its purposes is to help a man obtain a sense of perspective on the world and some view of himself with regard to his obligations to others. On the other hand, specific instruction in the mysteries of law, embalming, plumbing, medicine, holy orders, and business administration is vocational *training*. It has nothing to do with education. It is normally the province of a liberal arts college to deal with education, while training in trade skills is normally the province of the graduate schools of a university or may be had within on-the-job apprentice training programs.

Considered as a formal institution, college is a convenience in the acquisition of an education. It is never a determinant. Its courses are less important for the subject matter they discuss than for the discipline requisite to mastery of that subject matter. So the purpose of requiring courses in the natural sciences, the social sciences, and the humanities is not to fill a student's head with a few facts about the earthworm's metabolism, the Whisky Rebellion, and Milton, but to demand that he use his head in three different ways and learn a little respect for the academic disciplines in the process. Within a few years after graduation, nearly everyone will have forgotten almost every factual detail of the subjects he allegedly mastered, and no one expects him to remember them. But we do expect him to carry away from college a few first principles, a familiarity with the modes of thought and expression, an enduring concern for affairs of the mind,

23

respect for the truth and a knowledge of how to get at the truth of everyday affairs. There is nothing here that cannot be acquired elsewhere than in college at various times of one's life. College is merely the most convenient place to learn how to learn.

It is also a place where an adolescent can grow four years older. During this time, he may acquire a certain patina; perhaps he will acquire some appreciation of music, books, art, the theater, and politics. But then, he may not—for in the last analysis, all depends upon the student.

"Fundamentally, a college education will not change a person, if the person is strong, ambitious, motivated and able," the dean of admissions at one state university said. "These are qualities he will bring to the college with him. If he is not motivated, if he does not have integrity, a college education will not improve him."

In short, the dean said, a student will get out of college a value equal to the effort he puts into it—presuming, of course, that the college actually has something to offer the student. Mismatches can occur, as a later chapter will make clear.

With these thoughts in mind, let us now ask just what relevance a college education might have to the jobs in the workaday world. If we are going to mitigate the current hysteria attendant upon trying to wedge Jimmy into Yale, it would seem wise to assume that the *necessary* relevance of a college education to a job still remains to be proved—that common belief, or even common practice, is not proof enough.

For example, the argument can be made that a college education was *not* necessary to the success of my generation, which was the one that was graduated

24

from the nation's high schools during the Depression. In those days, not all of us went to high school. Of those who did, a minority chose the college preparatory courses. Of those who took such courses, not all went to college. In sum, most of us lack college diplomas. Yet, today, within any socioeconomic level, it is difficult to distinguish those of us who went to college from those of us who did not, for within any particular level, our style of life, intellectual interests, reading habits, social and political activity, and general outlook are virtually identical. Perhaps this reflects a sad failure on the part of the colleges to have done much for those of us who attended; perhaps it speaks well for those of us who did not. In any event, some of us who did not go to college earn much more, have accomplished more, and contribute more to society than some of us who hold degrees. It is true that most of us who went to college earn more money than most of us who did not, but there are a great many exceptions to this rule on both sides of the line. Fortunes have been made by men whose mental processes ranged from the rudimentary to the contemptible, while many who hold graduate degrees are content to live on minuscule academic salaries.

Possession of a college degree was therefore no guarantee of fame and fortune for us, nor, unfortunately, can all of us who hold degrees be regarded as educated men. Moreover, it is not always possible to say that our outstandingly successful college graduates owe their success solely to the fact that they went to college. Rather, it is more accurate to say that when they got out into the world, they merely continued to exhibit those qualities they had already begun to display in kindergarten.

With the history of our generation so obvious, why should there be such an insistence today that a college education is essential to success of any sort, or to obtaining what could, by any standards, be considered a good job? For instance, the Presidency of the United States might be considered a worthy occupation in several respects, but lack of a college education did not keep Harry S Truman out of the White House. To be a novelist is not always reprehensible, and one does not need to go to college to speak to the condition of man, as Mark Twain might have observed, or as Ernest Hemingway might have said when presented with the Nobel Prize for literature. I do not wish to argue the point from conspicuous exceptions, but merely wish to suggest that a college education has not been the sole means to a useful life in times past, and to suggest that not all of us who went to college became happier, wealthier, and more contributive citizens than those of us who spent our early youth doing something else.

Turning to the present day, we cannot say that a significant number of our current tasks are so complicated as to require a formal education, for this would presume that my generation is more highly educated than it actually is, or that the work we are doing is too sophisticated for us to handle. Except in the cases of our professional men—our doctors, lawyers, professors, and scientists in general—few of our college graduates can demonstrate the slightest connection between the daily demands of their jobs and what they studied in college. (Nor, for that matter, were our professional men's undergraduate educations always germane to their careers. Now, as then, acquiring a college diploma is just a kind of entrance fee—costing up to $12,000

26

at the better schools—that you must pay before they will let you into professional graduate schools.)

Looking to the future, we can easily see that the world's business will increasingly become a function of interdependent specialists; that automation will continue to deplete the number of jobs available to the entirely uneducated. It is predictable that, as far into the future as man may go, education will be asked to play an ever larger role, and that *some* kind of education, or training past high school, will be indispensable to the acquisition of an increasing proportion of the jobs that society will have to offer. But it is an open question whether this training, or education, must be had only in college. Nearly all less-than-professional tasks can best be learned on the job, to the great advantage of both employer and employee. There is no reason to believe this will not continue to be the case.

To be sure, some tasks might require some specific preliminary training simply as a convenience to an employer. For instance, the office secretary should know how to spell. In addition, she would be all the more welcome in an office if she also knew how to operate a digital computer—a skill that may be acquired quickly by anyone who has mastered arithmetic. But there is nothing that most secretaries do that would necessarily require them to become bachelors of the liberal arts at, say, Vassar, before they applied for their jobs. There will be nothing in the office routine that Vassar could teach them better, more rapidly, and less expensively than a secretarial school would. Even if knowledge of a particular skill—let us say, a foreign language—is essential to a private secretary's job, a college is not always the best place to

27

learn it. (Indeed, when it comes to languages, a college may be the worst place to learn.)

Similarly, there is nothing about being a salesman of life insurance that demands the salesman be a college graduate. His *training* for such a job could best be given him by his company. His general *education* may or may not have something to do with his performance on the job, but education is not a process confined to colleges.

Nowhere in the creative or communicative arts is a college diploma essential, although it might well be a convenience to the artist to have attended a school of fine arts. But no one wonders whether a painter has gone to school. Our interest is held by what he paints. We are interested in the sounds a musician makes— not in his formal education. Talented young men and women can find all sorts of employment in publishing houses, in magazine and newspaper offices, in the entertainment world, without having college degrees. A fast-growing area of employment is that comprising sales of goods and services related to outdoor recreation. Nowhere in this area is a college education an essential condition of employment. There are more than 20,000 different kinds of jobs offered in our society, and only a small fraction of them actually require specific college preparation. It would seem that the longer one considers the alleged relationship between job and diploma, the less real reason one finds for assuming there *is* a relationship between the content of a formal education and the humdrum demands of the daily work we actually do. If this is the case, are we being realistic when we say that a man must have a diploma to get a job? There might be reason to relate a college man's *training* with his employment, as in the case of a business college graduate who enters commerce. But here, a question arises as to how valuable that man's business courses were to him, and how germane they are to the particular business he enters. The day after his final college examinations, he has most usually forgotten the bulk of what he studied. But even if he remembers that course in Economics 309C he took three years ago, it might not apply to anything connected with his present employment in the pretzel industry.

When we come down to it, the only reason we believe that a man *must* have a college diploma to get a job nowadays is that everyone else seems to believe he should.

Please notice that we are being unrealistic when we insist that job applicants hold college degrees. For if we carried our belief to its logical extent, we would deny employment to 70 per cent of our high school graduates, for only 50 per cent of them now go to college, and of that 50 per cent, only 60 per cent finish. Therefore, to whatever extent employers demand diplomas of applicants, they push us all toward a practical impossibility.

It must be said that we are willing to be pushed, each of us fondly imagining that *our* youngsters will be among the lucky 30 per cent who win degrees. When we consider college admission, we do not often dwell upon a love of learning, or respect for scholarship, or a concern for affairs of the mind. We are more inclined to view college as the best of all marriage markets for our daughters and as the certain pathway to financial success for our sons, and so strongly do we hope, and believe, that we resort to almost any means to get them into college—often mortgaging our homes, impoverishing ourselves, changing our religions, pulling strings, and cheating in the process.

29

2

Bob:6,dean of admissions:0

College authorities like to believe that the freshmen
arriving on campus today have selected the colleges
they attend as carefully as the colleges have selected
them, and that the students are avid to learn what the
professors have to profess. For example, one Yale professor says that the helter-skelter days of Joe College,
Betty Coed, and the gentleman's C are dead. He delightedly believes that Yale students today are as
serious as they are bright.

Their intellectual curiosity and devotion to scholarship, he says, is demonstrated by their constant pres-
ence in the library; by their reading widely outside
their prescribed courses; by the mature interest they
take in attending debates, lectures by visiting luminar-
ies, musical and dramatic productions. The picture he
presented was one of a community devoted to affairs
of the mind, working purposefully toward worthy
ends.

30

"Today's kids," he concludes, "are wonderful."

Nothing would be more wonderful than if matters at Yale were precisely as the good professor describes them. Unfortunately, there are reasons to suspect that his view may be colored by wishful thinking. In saying this, I have no intention of denigrating either the professor, the student body, or Yale. But let us take a closer look at the Yale students:

The only thing they have in common is that they are all young and intelligent. They won admission to Yale partly on the basis of their scholastic aptitude test scores and partly on the basis of their success in the College Entrance Examination Board achievement tests in subject matter. No matter what one thinks of these tests, they are the currently standard means of measuring aptitude and achievement, and the Yale applicants' test scores are quite remarkable. A boy's admission to Yale is also partly based on his excellent high school academic record and partly on character references from his high school principal and teachers. In many cases, these references are bolstered by reports from Yale alumni who have interviewed the boy. By all possible means, Yale tries to fill its freshman class with a representative selection of the nation's potentially ablest scholars, of sterling character, who have already demonstrated outstanding academic and social achievement. Thus the boy who enters Yale is one that any college would be glad to have. He may have been president of his high school senior class, while also having been an honor student, three-letter athlete, editor of the literary magazine, and chairman of the student council; and his test scores may place him within the upper 1 per cent of the nation's rated academic aptitude and achievement for high school seniors in the year of his graduation. Such a glittering

31

figure is by no means uncommon on the campuses of colleges as selective as Yale.

All this says something about the boy, but it does not say enough. What does his apparent record really mean? Might he not merely be a good lesson learner who has not an original thought in his head? Why has he chosen Yale, apart from what he told his interviewers? We know he has academic aptitude and that he has proved that he can use it, but does he really care to use his keen mind on academic lumber *in college?* Perhaps he might now prefer to do something else. After all, in any population of intelligent people, the number who prefer a life of action is always greater than the number of those who prefer a life of scholarship.

How many of those boys in the library are there simply because they must read books to pass courses? How many who attend the extracurricular activities do so because they find them more interesting than the required work? How serious a scholar must one be to earn top marks at Yale? How interested in learning is he who says he intends to enter graduate school and become a teacher? How accurately do those character references describe a boy's character? Is there not always the chance that they are somewhat hastily formed on the basis of whatever face a clever boy has chosen to present to adult strangers? When a Yale boy joins a freedom march, does this always mean intellectual commitment? Is not any eighteen-year-old freshman, no matter how bright, also a jumble of hopes, confusions, doubts, torments, dreams, and gaucheries, whirling around a storm center of incandescent sexuality? How is the good professor's roseate view of a campus full of industrious intellectuals to be equated with a

riot between Yale students and New Haven policemen, or the vandalism of someone's house at a debu-
tante party, or with that fine old Yale tradition of
sticking one's bare backside out a dormitory window?

Listen for a moment to the voices of several Yale
students, remembering that what they tell us may be
no more accurate a reflection of their real thoughts
than what they tell any other adult:

"I'm here because my father said he wouldn't pay
the bill if I went anywhere else."

"If I can stay in college and graduate school until
I'm married, or twenty-six, I'll get out of the draft."

"I know teachers don't make any money, but you
get the summer off. Besides, there's enough money
in the family to see me through college, and by the
time I'm teaching, money won't matter any more because my aunt's about dead now, and she's *loaded*."

"What else would I do for the next four years? Join
the Army?"

"I want to be with my friends, and all my friends are
in college."

"If you're not Ivy, you're out of it."

"If there's one thing we're all good at, it's the interview. That's why we're here. All you have to do is
figure out what the clods want to hear. You play it
straight-arrow, and they all go ape and eat it up. You
don't think they're going to disagree with their own
ideas, do you?"

"My girl signed up for Connecticut [Connecticut
College for Women]. I wanted to go to a good school,
close to hers."

"Yale was really my second choice, but they answered first, and we panicked."

The examples could be multiplied, but only to

33

further the suggestion that at least some Yale students may not be entirely sure just why they are there; that their reasons for attendance may not always be the best in the world; that they are somewhat resentful of the process that got them there; that some really do not know what they are doing, and that more than a few have no interest whatsoever in serious scholarship. The same things can be said of any student body in any college in the land.

Surely, we cannot put too much credence in what may often be the prattle of boys, but this is just the point: They are *boys*. They may be academically bright boys, but they are often little lost boys in a Never Never Land that they do not wholly understand. Yale may indeed have many undergraduates who came for good reasons, knowing exactly what they wanted Yale to do for them, and who have found matters congruent with their expectations. But unless Yale is remarkably different from all other selective colleges, the majority of its students are there not because they know why, or because they want to study anything in particular, but *essentially because there is no longer any socially acceptable place except college in our society for bright boys between eighteen and twenty-two years old*, and because the brightest of the bright are encouraged, enticed, persuaded, badgered, hounded, ordered, and driven to try to get into places like Yale.

Think for a moment about the eighteen- to twenty-two-year-old, and it will at once be apparent that his position in our society is anomalous. He may be engaging, full of fun, and wonderful in many ways. He may even have some marketable skills. He certainly has an adult body and adult desires. We nonetheless think him half-baked. We say he lacks practical experi-

ence, lacks knowledge, lacks insight. We say he is not
yet emotionally or economically ready for marriage;
and although he is sexually more potent than he will
ever be again, we tell him he cannot, or should not,
have sex outside of marriage. At eighteen and out of
high school, he is far and away more mature—in all
senses of the word—than the high school freshman
of fourteen, but he is just as far from being accepted
as a responsible citizen. Once he is out of high school
we rather assume that he no longer has any problems
that he cannot solve. In any event, we are not eager
to solve them for him, arguing that it is high time he
grew up. But how is he to gain experience, and where
is he to grow up? These youths comprise the great
bulk of the nation's unemployed. Employers do not
want them; labor unions do not want them; we do not
want them hanging around the house. The military
services would be glad to have them, but who in times
of peace stops to think that the Army might be a good
place for a bright boy, and that we are able to enjoy
what we have only because intelligent warriors protect
us? Rather than encourage our youth to enlist, we
most often tell them that military service is an un-
fortunate waste of a young man's time. We are unwilling for our young almost-men to be allowed to run
loose, although in some cases, just such freedom would
be more beneficial to particular boys than entering
college immediately after high school.

In sum, the eighteen- to twenty-two-year-old is a
problem to us, but if he is bright, then we think the
solution is to ship our problem off to college. There,
out of sight and mind, he can grow four years older
without great harm to himself or to others. He will
have a good time, and it makes us feel good to be able

to send him there. Sometimes, the more of a financial sacrifice it is for us, the better it makes us feel. College, we commonly say, never hurt anyone, and even if Johnny doesn't yet know what he wants to do in life, he will perhaps learn something useful, or find something interesting in college, although we certainly do not want him to turn into an egghead. If he does well in college, we are glad to take credit for his success. If he fails, or quits, we can say that it was not our fault.

To be sure, there are many reasons why we send our children to college besides our simple desire to get them out of the house, but this is one of the important reasons. The result of an entire catalogue of reasons is that more than half of our high school graduates now go on to college, and because of *this*, a college education is no longer the privilege it once was for an earlier generation. Rather, *going to college has merely become the general activity of the intelligent young, to whom we offer nothing else.* Contributing a paper to Nevitt Sanford's book, *The American College,* David Riesman and Christopher Jencks put the matter thus:

"The American college exists as a vast WPA project which gives promising adolescents work to do while keeping them out of the job market and also keeping several hundred thousand faculty members off the streets."

Within this WPA project, parents, colleges, and students have evolved a sort of unwritten scale of values by which to measure themselves and each other with respect to college admission.

For instance, young people who go to college are prone to regard those who do not as "clods, animals" and "yo-yos." They say "the clods are out of it." Then, picking up what they hear around the house, at school, and in great measure from the colleges themselves, they assign places in a pecking order. It varies with geography. For example, it is considered perfectly proper—in California—for a bright boy to say he wants to go to Stanford. But if a bright Philadelphia boy should say *he* wants to go to Stanford, a great many of his classmates would assume it is because the boy knows he cannot hope to get into a *good* school. In the East, the general belief is that there are no good schools ("not really good") anywhere else. This snobbish view includes the notion that most of the Eastern schools are second-rate, but that Southern and Western schools are third-rate, with second-rate exceptions. Thus, a Philadelphia boy might say:

"Oh, sure, Stanford's better than Penn State, but who goes to Penn State except the kind of guys who go to Temple, or Boston College?"

And his sister might say to another girl:

"If he goes to Harvard, he must be a brain; if he goes to Miami, he's stupid; if he goes to some place like Oberlin, for God's sake, he isn't anybody you'd really want to know. Swarthmore is for beatniks, and Yale is tall, strong, and dumb. Frankly, I'd take Dartmouth—he won't be too bright and he'll like a good time."

The girl to whom this code is addressed will have no difficulty deciphering it as follows:

Harvard is exclusively populated by insufferable intellectuals with whom ordinary discourse is impossible. Miami University in Florida is perhaps libelously known as Suntan U. The presumption among urban East Coast children is that no one goes to Miami unless (a) he just wants to swim and (b) he cannot gain entrance to any other university. Oberlin, like Kenyon and Lawrence, is regarded as "one of those small schools out in the middle of nowhere" that is trying to attract a good student body and build a reputation, but so far has not succeeded. (As one Eastern girl said, "All right, they want good kids. But who wants to be the pioneer? Who would you talk to if you went there?") Swarthmore is regarded as good, but raffish: "Those kids are too far out." Yale and Dartmouth are quite respectable, as all Ivy League colleges are, but it is felt that a Yale boy is an unexciting sort "who goes into business," and that Dartmouth boys "get bombed out of their minds." The University of Pennsylvania is regarded as the bottom of the Ivies ("you're just barely in"), and for this reason it suffers from an acute, and interesting, admissions problem we shall presently discuss.

The important fact about such offhand opinions is not that they may be wholly false, slanderous, and unfair. Rather, it is that they are so widely held. While the various sections of the country may entertain specifically different views of the various colleges, all of these views will be cut of the same cloth. Although no one can seriously contend that any great university could possibly consist of just one sort of student, we tend to think of a university as if it did.

The poisonous thing about type-casting is that it tends to be a self-fulfilling process. One result is that a college will attract students not on the basis of whatever studies it offers, but on the basis of the presumed characteristics of its student body, to the point where the college actually does come to resemble its public image. University authorities speak of the process as "preselection." By this, they mean that a

38

bright student, who knows that his marks and test scores would qualify him for admission to any college, will pick one on grounds that he will there meet many students like himself, imagining that all other factors are equal among good colleges. "There will be more of my kind of guys," he will say. Thus, while it is far from Reed College's desire to become known as the Bohemia of the West Coast, populated by enormously intelligent but emotionally intense short-haired girls and long-haired boys, who both wear war surplus combat jackets, sandals, and bathing shorts to class, just enough Reed students of this sort exist to give the college a caricature, with the result that Reed receives a large proportion of entrance applications from youngsters who run to the type.

Selection by caricature, however indefensible, is perhaps the predominant reason for most applications to certain selective colleges. It is also about as good a reason as any other that most applicants tell their parents, high school, and college deans of admission. Not to put too fine a point on it, most of the stated reasons are lies.

For example, if Bob says he wants to go to Dartmouth "because they have a good math department, and I will probably major in math," the chances are that he is merely giving us a parent-society–pleasing answer. To see what inspired it, let us visit the principal of a large city high school, who describes an unfortunately typical situation:

"Kids don't really know the college, and they can't know," the principal said. "They won't know what college is actually like until they go there and live there.

"The high school guidance officer has X hundred

kids to advise, and he has never taught them in class," the principal continued. "He knows them only as figures on form sheets. He meets the kid and the kid's parents for the first time at the counseling session. All he knows about them is what is on the form sheet on his desk. He sees them for the first time, and then and there, in fifteen minutes, he is supposed to say something that will affect a human being's entire future life.

"What is he to say? He knows no more than the kids, as to what the colleges are like, because *he* hasn't been to the colleges, either. The only college he knows anything about may be the teachers college he attended years ago, and that college has materially changed since he was there. All he knows about the colleges is what he reads on another form sheet: At such-and-such U, the average SAT and CEEB scores of the incoming freshmen class is thus-and-so. Ink and paper facts; not living, three-dimensional facts.

"So," the principal said, "the kid and his parents and the guidance officer all solemnly sit there and talk about something none of them know anything about other than by hearsay, on the basis of figures that may have no relevance to the boy in question. The officer checks the kid's record and says, 'On your grades and scores, you could go to this, this, or this college. Why not apply here? You have a good math aptitude; you might want to major in math.' And the kid says, 'Yes, but I don't want to go to school here in this state. I want to go to some new part of the country. Does Dartmouth have a good math department?' And the guidance officer says, 'Dartmouth is an excellent school.'"

Whereupon, all is decided, and a public myth is

40

born: the boy utters a pious little lie, knowing how badly everyone wants to believe it. What he does *not* tell the guidance officer, his parents, or Dartmouth, but what he may confide to his friends, is that older boys have told him that weekends at Mt. Holyoke are "a real blast." Wherefore, he intends to spend every available weekend there, and Dartmouth seems a reasonable base for his operations, because he also likes to ski. If he flatly said, "I want to go to Dartmouth to ski, and because it is close to Mt. Holyoke," he would shortly learn the hazards of telling the truth—viz., Dartmouth wouldn't accept him.

The colleges themselves encourage this pretense, no doubt unwittingly, by virtue of their insistence that they are communities of scholars, and that applicants give intellectual reasons for wishing to attend. Since there is such a pressure put on young people to go, and for colleges to operate at capacity, the result is hypocrisy on both sides. The applicants pretend to be scholars, and the colleges pretend to believe them.

Surely, no professor can look at the mass of incoming students, no matter how bright the mass may be, and say with a straight face that all of them are keenly motivated scholars. If he did, he would probably be deceiving himself, if not us, because there is ample research to suggest that scholarly motivation is *not* the reason most boys go to college, nor is it the reason why most girls attend. The U.S. Office of Education flatly says that most boys go to college in belief this will help them get jobs, and that most girls go in hope of finding husbands.

While these reasons may be as sound as any others for going to school, they are almost never told by applicants to deans of admission. But in the light not only of common knowledge, but also of expert research, it would seem impossible, or naïve, for the deans not to know that what the applicants say on admission forms is said for the record, and that what is said for the record is often somewhat less than candid.

For that matter, what the colleges tell the applicants may sometimes be far from the truth. Robert Iffert tells of a college recruiter "who goes around to all the high schools making his institution seem to be all things to all men, telling a boy there is a program of nuclear physics when, as a matter of fact, there isn't one. . . ."

Mr. Iffert's remark brings up a curious aspect of the business of admission. At the very time that our selective colleges turn away well-qualified applicants for reasons of lack of space, they send talent scouts throughout the land to try to sell high school students, and their parents, on the virtue of attending dear old Amherst, Harvard, or Wherever. "College night" for parents and students is a fixture of contemporary high school life, with some schools holding these meetings for the benefit of audiences as young as that of the tenth grade.

The usual procedure is for several personable young men from the admissions offices of different colleges to hold forth from the auditorium stage, each speaking to the virtues of his school and subsequently answering questions put by the audience. After the formal meeting, the young men may be found in the gymnasium, sitting behind card tables piled with college brochures and bulletins, ready to talk turkey with interested customers.

During the formal session, the college representa-

tives will make the point that though it is true that the
selective colleges are oversubscribed by gifted applicants, there are so many colleges in the land that there
is sure to be some kind of college that will have space
for your child. True, they will say, your son may not
be accepted at *our* school, because . . . well, frankly,
because we are better than most schools, and we take
none but the very best. But there are, they will say
with infinite condescension, quite a number of really
good little liberal arts schools out in the Midwest.
From what they say, and the way they say it, one
instantly gathers that attendance at any of those good
little schools is an admission of partial failure, and that
beneath those schools yawns a foul pit, at the bottom
of which lies the state university.

The reason for this assiduous talent search in a
seller's market is that the selective colleges rate themselves on the basis of the intelligence, aptitude, and
achievement levels of their incoming freshmen classes
and on the scholarly prestige and publications of their
professors. Wherefore they beat the high school bushes
for talented students as vigorously as any football
coach looking for quick halfbacks; and with equal
spirit they raid rival faculties for prestigious professors.
On the face of it, there might seem nothing wrong
with the idea of any college trying to be the best college there is, but there are grounds for believing that
this activity is being overdone to a point that is detri-
mental to the best interests of the students, the colleges themselves, and the nation in general.

For instance, the personable young college repre-
sentatives are salesmen who sell their product on the
basis of intellectual snobbery. As a result, the selective
colleges exacerbate the very conditions they publicly

deplore: selection by caricature, and an almost maniacal anxiety on the part of parents to somehow jam their children into the most prestigious schools. A further result is that the selective colleges tend to silt up, as one Reed professor said, "with an academic elite of arrogant young snips."

No one who has ever watched a mixed group of college youngsters meet socially can doubt that lines have been drawn. The boys and girls from the Ivy League and the Heavenly Seven women's colleges are, by and large, easily distinguished from the rest. Other students will regard them with anything ranging from frustrated envy to a sort of rueful awe, and before the evening is well under way, the youngsters will have split into separate groups. To speak in terms of caricature, the Ivy League will be talking with its own members, throwing occasional tidbits to those who attend Haverford and Carleton. The Kenyon-Pomona axis will be found in another corner of the room, while the state university people will mill around in the middle of the floor with those from Duke, Houston, and Hofstra.

There is simply no question that the admissions practices tend to confirm an academic elite in our society, and the only remaining question is whether this is good. Some parents (usually those whose children are safely ensconced in the Ivy League) will say there is nothing wrong with a process of natural selection based on survival of the fittest, arguing, "Well, a kid is going to have to find out sooner or later that he can't cut the mustard, and he might as well get used to it early." This view, even if valid, does not embrace the plight of those who were perfectly well qualified for admission to the selective colleges but who were refused simply because there was not room enough for all who were qualified. There is evidence that such youngsters have some difficulty arriving at a separate peace with life:

At the University of Chicago, for example, a group of boys call themselves "Harvard rejects." By this, they do not mean that Harvard threw them out, but rather, that Harvard had not accepted them. They hold themselves to be superior to their fellow students at Chicago because, as one of them said, "At least we were good enough to *apply* for Harvard, which is more than you can say for the rest of the guys here."

Their presumption of superiority is not borne out by their grade averages, nor by any other objective criteria, but the point is that their disappointment is genuine and their outlook sour.

And at the University of Pennsylvania there is "the problem of the prep school boy," which one Penn professor explained thus:

"These are the boys who have gone to good private schools, and who come from families with a university tradition, but who were not accepted at Princeton, Harvard, or Yale, and who feel they must go to an Ivy League college. They feel that by coming to Penn, they only reached second base, instead of making a home run."

He said these boys take the attitude that since Penn is presumed to be the bottom of the Ivy League the courses cannot be difficult, and that they can sit back and breeze through on the basis of no work. So they let their work pile up, or slide by, until they are in real academic difficulty. Whereupon, they either quit, or flunk out of a school they hadn't really wanted to attend in the first place and which they erroneously regarded as being beneath them.

Penn's problem with the prep school boy stems from

the fact that no test has been devised that can determine whether a boy *will want to do college work.* On the basis of the application forms, Penn knows only that these boys are well qualified. Their aptitude and achievement scores on the College Entrance Examination Board tests may be in the high 600's; their prep school records will be excellent. But Penn can never know how many prep school boys have actually chosen Penn for good reasons, and which of them have merely clutched at Penn as a sort of last straw. The only thing Penn knows for sure is that a public high school boy with comparable test scores is more likely to stay in college than are the private school boys who apply to Penn. On the other hand, given a choice between admitting a prep school boy with high test scores and a public school boy with low ones, Penn would feel constrained to take the boy with the better scores because no one can be sure that the prep school boy is not serious, and on the record, he is the stronger candidate. The result is that Penn has wretched luck with a disproportionate number of the private school boys it admits.

Smith College president Thomas Mendenhall said he believes that a central problem of college admission stems from the fact that many parents and high school students put more thought on the ways and means of getting into a college than they put on trying to find out what college is all about, or what the student will do, once there. As we have seen, some students apply to a college because either they, or their parents, think that admission to a good school gives them, and the whole family, a superior social status—a view that does not always bespeak a strong concern for affairs of the mind, nor a realistic appraisal of the qualities of the

46

applicant. Painfully familiar to high school principals are those students who join a great many extracurricular committees and clubs with no intention of actually participating in the several activities, but rather because they believe "it will look good on my college application if they see I went out for a lot of other stuff." Just as familiar is the high school parent who says he helps his child with the homework "because if I don't help him, his grades won't be good enough to get him into a good college."

This undue concern for admission (as contrasted with a lesser concern for what educational values a particular college might offer a particular applicant) is sharpened not only by the salesmanship of the college recruiters who visit the high schools, but also by certain practices of the high schools themselves. For example, some high schools give explicit directions to their students.

"When you go to the dean's office for your interview," one principal tells his students, "be sure you have read the college bulletin, so that you can tell the dean you know his college offers such-and-such a course and that you are interested in that field and would like to sit in on the class while you're there visiting the college."

Given a serious student, there is nothing wrong with such advice. Unfortunately, most high school students in today's special world of pressure construe the principal's remark to mean that it is all a game you play with the dean; that this is just a clever way of making the dean think favorably of you. Within the particular context of the high school I have in mind, such a deduction happens to be entirely accurate, for the school exists in a college-oriented suburban community and the principal has considerable reason to believe that his job depends upon the number of students he can get into colleges. In short, the students deduce that they are to pretend—and pretense might strike some people as a rather unpromising basis upon which to build a higher education.

Yet a certain amount of pretense would seem inescapable, inasmuch as few high school students can have any personal knowledge or experience of college life or college work at the particular institution to which they apply as their "first choice"; much less have most students any intellectual reason to prefer one college they know nothing about to another college that they know nothing about. On the other hand, as Bob's application to Dartmouth suggests, many students do have quite genuine, if unimpressive, reasons for their college preferences.

One of the real reasons, as simple as it is genuine, is proximity. The dean of admissions at one state university said that most students at his school come from homes within an 80-mile radius of the campus. He said some will privately admit that the reason for their choice of college was that they lacked money enough to go anywhere else. But this attribution, he said, is almost in every case without merit; it is most often a convenient, unchallengable excuse.

"What they are really saying," he ventured, "is that they have no reasons of their own for attendance other than a general feeling that they should, or must, go to college now that they are out of high school, and this being the case, the closest college will do."

Another reason for preference, just as genuine as proximity, is distance.

"I wanted to come here," one student at Berkeley

said, "because it's 2,000 miles away from my house, and because my old man wanted me to go to Princeton, just like every other idiot in my family did."

Another perfectly genuine reason for preference was expressed by a girl who rejected Smith in favor of Cornell, saying "I wanted to go to a co-ed school, because at an all-girl school, the kids get grubby from Monday to Friday."

Now of course it is good for many a boy to want to get away from the home town. To rebel against a father is only natural; to prefer a co-educational school to another kind should be a legitimate option. The point to be made about these statements is, not that they are not genuine expressions of honest emotions, but that they are not the kind of reasons that a serious scholar might advance for his attendance at a particular university. But why should they be? The great majority of our high school students who go to college will never be serious scholars, although every student accepted at one of our highly selective colleges has the ability to carve out a scholarly career for himself if he wishes to do so. At the moment of college entrance, however, the incoming freshman is usually a veritable innocent whose going to college is more normally a process of his being led, or pushed into it, than it is a matter of thoughtful choice related to intellectual ambitions realistically formed on a basis of personal analysis. As Robert Iffert says, "Youngsters have practically nothing systematic in their reasons for going to college."

But then, as he also says, "They often have purpose, order, and design in their reasons for leaving." As we shall see in Chapter 8, no less than 60 per cent of all students who enter college will either flunk out, drop out, or transfer out of the colleges of their choice.

3

Look who's teaching
them now

When a high school student leaves home for college
today, he thinks he is about to enter heaven. Everyone
has told him that college entrance is the chief goal of
adolescent life, that once admitted he will be safe for
ever and ever. True, some students experience a pleas-
ant thrill of fear as they set off, but all carry with them
the exhilarating notion that they are about to en-
counter some massive experience that will affect their
lives for the better. A few months later, the more
thoughtful of them will have concluded that going
to college and acquiring an education are not necessarily synonymous, and that if college is heaven, then
heaven could certainly stand a few radical improve-
ments.

"Any school that has fraternities, drum majorettes,
and a marching band can't be too great," one college
boy said from his experience. "You just *know* it's going
to be full of Mickey Mouse."

50

Freely translated, Mickey Mouse means pointless trivia. The student's remarks reflected his opinion that any student body that would support fraternities and marching bands could not be an intellectual one, and that being the case, the academic work offered at the college must necessarily be piffling.

Mickey Mouse also means busywork, or childishly simple studies puffed thin and served up with mind-numbing pretense. An example would be a course in teaching driver training which the author observed at one teachers college. A learned doctor of the arts of transportation displayed a yellow octagonal sign to his lecture-hall audience. It was lettered STOP.

"This is a stop sign," he explained.

"When you see this sign, what must you do?" he asked.

"You must come to a complete stop," he answered himself.

On he went, explaining in detail that the driver must —if he is driving an automobile with a pedal-operated clutch—be sure to disengage the clutch and move the gear shift lever into neutral position as he slows to a complete halt. Next, the driver should look first to the left, then to the right. If the intersection was clear, then the driver could proceed across it, first synchronizing foot and hand to engage the clutch into low gear, sufficiently accelerating the engine to prevent stalling; shifting into higher gears as the automobile gained speed.

Then the good doctor explained the entire process all over again with respect to the stopping and starting of an automobile that had hydraulically operated gears.

Through all of this, his audience of twenty-year-old students solemnly took notes.

51

Professors of the liberal arts tend to regard teachers colleges as veritable cloud banks of Mickey Mouse, and they are often derisive of degrees granted by schools of education. Yet, their own houses may not be in perfectly scrupulous order, since crumbs of knowledge from any field can, upon occasion, be blown up into preposterous wedding cakes at even the best of universities. As one Harvard boy said, "A kid can float through here on gut courses if all he wants is the degree."

The fact that such a thing is possible can infuriate an idealistic boy, who with the intolerance of youth will promptly decide that the whole business of obtaining a degree is a sick farce, and that his sense of honor will not permit him to remain a party to it.

It is particularly easy for the bright product of a sophisticated high school to come to such a conclusion in a state university that has minimal entrance requirements. At such schools, the undergraduate courses are apt to seem thin to him, and the worthwhile courses will seem to have been reserved for the graduate school. For example, let us sit in on a class at one of those universities:

It is a class in sophomore English, and a young man we will call John Gray is holding forth on Browning. Dr. Gray is a newly minted assistant professor, only slightly older than his students. He is the one sitting on the desk in front of the room, swinging his legs, pushing a raven forelock higher on his brow as he lectures.

"The modular intensity of Browning's words forms a shifting, always-changing skein upon which his thoughts play as light birds against a garden wall—as glimmers against a mystery—as they flit from some unimaginable beginning to stand for a moment, then fly to some unimaginable end."

Dr. Gray happens to be quoting from his dissertation, entitled *A Structural Analysis of Five Poems by Robert Browning with Particular Reference to Certain Uses of Modular Intensity.* The title is in every way descriptive of the dissertation, and in my opinion, speaks volumes about the graduate school that granted Dr. Gray his Ph.D.

"Browning/obscure," Tom Swift, one of the boys in a back seat, had written in his notebook half an hour ago. The rest of Tom's page consists of little gallows and geometric designs. Now, as Dr. Gray pauses, Tom writes again. "Eng. tr.—B. can't write and/or G. eats it." Moodily, Tom crosses everything out and yawns.

"Sliding walls and birds v. important to B.," Mary Carswell adds to her page of neat lines of flawless script. "He is v. mysteryious and beautifull."

By "He" Mary does not really mean Browning, but rather, Dr. Gray. This is a fact of which Mary is not yet aware. In fact, she is not particularly aware of much of anything. Her perfect script does not denote an orderly mind, but as is so often the case, an empty one. Ever since first grade, Mary has had trouble spelling, but she is what teachers call a good lesson learner. She takes copious notes because she always tries to remember everything her teachers say in order that she might agree with them. She passes because the true-false and multiple-choice examinations, both in high school and now in this enormous diploma mill, always contain sufficient hints to suggest the desired answer to her immediate memory. She can always remember just enough, for just long enough, to pass the tests. Whereupon, her mind reverts to its pristine innocence, and Mary is perfectly prepared, as a newly erased blackboard is prepared, for her next course. Her written work might leave some things to be desired, such as originality, perception, and style; but it is always on time, lengthy, and at least derives from the assignment. (Perhaps it is fortunate for her grade average, if not for her, that written examinations and assignments are few at this university. They are few because the classes are so large that instructors cannot thoroughly read and evaluate written work without adding hours to their work weeks—a condition that also prevailed at Mary's high school.) No one worries about Mary's spelling. No one ever has. In short, she was a fairly typical B student in her Midwestern high school, and now at her state's university, she continues to earn her Bs. She plans to major in English, rather vaguely feels she will someday be a writer, and almost certainly will join a ladies' reading club when she becomes a placid matron in some flaccid Milwaukee suburb.

Among other students in the class is Steve Ball, a quiet, self-sufficient Negro from New York City who regards the university with patient tolerance. He is there to get a degree; he is prepared to put up with anything to get that degree; he keeps his thoughts to himself while handing in work that reflects his professors' opinions; he is marking time until he can enter graduate school. His marks are straight A's except for this class with Dr. Gray, in which he is a C student. Steve's trouble is that he cannot always guess what Dr. Gray might be trying to say, with the result that he sometimes ventures original ideas. Then there is Jon Webster, who takes none of his work seriously, but who is having a fine time at the university. He is skating along on Cs and Ds, but vastly enjoying the fraternity he joined, knowing perfectly well that college is the one opportunity in a man's life to spend four years having a good time before having to go to work. There is also Bill Damon, the All-American line backer.

While there is no point in following this class in greater detail, it is instructive to talk with Dr. Gray at the end of the day. In conversation, we learn that Dr. Gray is just as unaware of the truth about Mary as he is unable to explain Browning either to himself or to anyone else. He believes that Mary likes his course, that romantic poetry deeply stirs her. True, Dr. Gray is sometimes shaken by the kind of questions Mary often asks, for it seems odd to him that anyone who listens so carefully, and takes so many notes, could so entirely have missed the point. Yet of all his students, Mary comes most often to him after class, and Dr. Gray believes this practice, and the light in her blue eyes, bespeaks nothing but a genuine thirst for learning. Like most teachers, he is prejudiced in favor of those who seem most eager and hopes they will be inspired to go on to graduate school to become teachers like himself.

But as for the unspeakable Tom Swift! Just as much of the B he gives Mary is his tribute to her attitude, so much of the D that Dr. Gray gives Tom reflects Dr. Gray's personal feelings about anyone who would have the gall to hand him a mid-term paper entitled *Byron, Shelley, and Keats—Edgar Guests in the Ode House.* There is no doubt that Tom is clever, but his cleverness has a sour, mean twist to it; his humor is sardonic rather than Homeric. Worst of all he is argumentative, and more than once Dr. Gray has found himself sprawling headfirst into one of Tom's logical pitfalls.

While Dr. Gray can take Jon Webster in stride, accurately measuring his man, Steve Ball is an enigma. Dr. Gray feels badly about Steve. He is secretly worried whether the C he gives Steve reflects an antipathy to Negroes, which would be disgraceful in a teacher, or whether it is just that Steve, because of his limited cultural background, is incapable of appreciating poetry. As for big Bill Damon, "Well," Dr. Gray will tell you, "he is a football player, as you know. The university policy is—and there is merit to this, don't you think—that since varsity athletes have such physical demands made on them, it would be unfair to mark them on the same scale with other students who don't have to expend the same energy."

The class we have just visited is typical only of itself —not of the nation, nor even of classes in that particular state university. The point is that Dr. Gray's class is just an example of what can happen to an innocent student who comes wandering into the school looking for an education. We shall presently see why this is so, but it is first important to understand that classes and teachers in a great state university present an educational spectrum as broad as that presented by the nation itself. Elsewhere in Dr. Gray's university— and in many others in this land—there will be classes of students who can boast no better than an eighth-grade reading level as determined by national standard tests, and the subject matter held out to such students will smack even more of Mickey Mouse than Dr. Gray's offering does. Yet, elsewhere in that same university, there are other classes where brilliant teachers with something to say invite the cut and thrust of argument with gifted students. There are teachers who will be no party to the conspiracy to keep varsity athletes eligible at any cost to honor, and these teachers will be well known to the coaches, with the result that no athletes are ever scheduled for their classes. As the dean of admissions of this university said, "As enrollment increases, the university has no choice but to accommodate itself to the achievement levels and capabilities of the students that our high schools send us. But I will say this: we are prepared to challenge the best they send here."

To dwell for a moment longer on Dr. Gray, it will be seen that he has no clear idea who his students really are, and that he is given to quoting his dissertation from memory and to believing not only that he is saying something worth hearing but that it makes sense to any student willing to apply himself. In all charity, Dr. Gray cannot be blamed for the error of his ways, for no one has ever told him what to do, or how to do it, and no one ever checks on what he does. He illustrates the truth of what Robert Iffert said in conversation:

"In terms of establishing a profession on the basis of preparation," Mr. Iffert said, "you might say there is no profession so unprofessional, so nonprofessional, as the professor's profession. He has less training for his profession than a bricklayer has for his trade. To say that having been taught qualifies you to teach, is a dubious assumption."

He said his Office of Education study of college dropouts "shows that while the students were not, ah, extremely critical of the faculty, their discouragement, dissatisfaction, stemmed from the fact that they couldn't get close to the teacher; that they and the teacher were living in different worlds. This is a bad situation, particularly in the large universities, where too much of the instruction is being carried on by graduate students whose purpose in being there is to get their doctorate and whose teaching is just a chore they perform along the way. Their inclination is to try out their dissertation on the students, and since the instructor's classroom is his castle, nobody is checking on him, and this is the thing that goes on. A significant number of able students who go to large institutions are dissatisfied particularly with the quality of the teaching and size of classes. The existence of such dissatisfaction does not augur well for the future, when increased enrollments may increase the number of large classes."

Among the most dissatisfied are the graduates of the handful of excellent private or public high schools who discover freshman year—even at many selective colleges—to be largely a rehash of work they have already mastered. Were they to attend a nonselective state university, they might well find all four undergraduate years to be a meager challenge.

Much of the trouble here stems from the uneven quality of the nation's high schools. No college can presume that all of its incoming freshman have had what the college might consider an adequate high school preparation to be, with the result that its first-year studies may be more in the nature of remedial education than anything else. For example, Harvard accepts nothing but the cream of the annual high school class. But Harvard says in a letter to parents of freshmen that most boys coming to Harvard will not have had adequate preparation in English composition. Wherefore, Harvard demands a course in composition in freshman year, and much of Harvard's first-year offerings in other disciplines will simply add up to a body of work that is largely available at a good preparatory school. To be sure, Harvard makes exceptions, placing advanced students in advanced courses, permitting some boys to enter as sophomores. But most colleges are not so flexible, nor in later years anywhere near so rigorous, and when a bright boy from an excellent preparatory school is required as a freshman to undertake a high school curriculum all over again, he is apt to quit in disgust before making some effort to find out what else the college might offer in its upper classes. A general truth here is that *all* students will find *something* disenchanting about the colleges they enter, but that those who remain to be graduated will be those who are able to stomach their disappointments, usually through discovery of some study or activity that more than compensates for what irritates them.

Perhaps the most cruelly disappointed are those serious students who enter a large, highly selective university because of the reputation of its senior professors. Here, they think, they will have an opportunity to learn from great men. On arrival, they discover that the great men will have nothing to do with them.

"I have no intention of wasting my time with freshmen," one full professor said. "It would not be an economical employment of my abilities, either from my point of view, or from that of the university."

Another professor, the world's leading authority in his field and the brightest ornament of a distinguished faculty, refuses to teach undergraduates. He reserves his knowledge for the benefit of no more than seven graduate students a year.

59

"The man with the most prestige around here," one professor said, "is one who doesn't teach a soul. He is too busy running around the country giving lectures, writing speeches for the governor, acting as a consultant to private industry or to the Defense Department, or looking for another college to pay him more money. Why do we want him? Because he is good advertising. I don't know whether his salary comes out of the advertising budget, but it should. We have him to bait the customers in; so that we can put his name in the bulletin, and say 'Here, at *our* school, *we* have Dr. Zilch, the world's foremost authority on buttercups.' "

Their dreams of walking and discoursing with Socrates having been shattered by reality, the incoming students of serious intent may, as noted, next be confronted with a schedule of courses that seem only too familiar, through which they will be guided by graduate students who serve as instructors. A professor explained the situation thus:

"Let's face it," he said, "you may have nobody but graduate students as your classroom teachers for your first two years. Your teachers may be only four years older than you are, which raises an interesting point:

"Every year since the war, each freshman class has been generally brighter and better prepared than the last. That story about how some of the professors wouldn't be admitted as freshmen, if they applied for entrance today, isn't a joke. We sent the credentials of one of our English professors through the admissions mill, under an assumed name, and he was turned down. Now, what does this mean? It means that your graduate instructors probably have lower IQs and lower aptitude and achievement test scores than you have. They might have gone to worse high schools. You've entered a selective college, and they might have gone to some cow college for their undergraduate degrees. If you come from a good Eastern private school, like Exeter, and your instructors went to dumb public high schools and so-so colleges, you might already have a better general education than they have. But *these* are the characters who are going to grade your work. Some have never taught school a day in their lives before you walked in, but so help me, they're your judge and jury. You thought you were coming to a top college full of top professors. Well, it's a top *university*, but the undergraduate college is something else, and if you want our good professors, you'll have to wait for graduate school, although you may get one or two in junior year."

At this point, we might understand why some students say they feel that being taught by graduate students represents a kind of fraud. Here they—and their families—are paying out thousands of dollars for a college education, much as they might have paid high prices for good seats at a national championship professional football game, only to discover that they are not to watch the stars play the game, but that the teams today are using their second- or third-string substitutes. The high school student trying to decide where to go to college is well-advised to study the college bulletins if he wishes to be exposed to the maximum number of professors during his undergraduate years. The bulletins will state who teaches what. From them, students will discover that some colleges—particularly the small, selective schools like Haverford—make a point of having professors in the undergraduate classrooms while in large universities (Harvard, for one) a student can wait until junior year before encountering a resident Socrates.

As indicated by the example of Dr. Gray, however, possession of a degree is no guarantee of educational ability, but it is at least suggestive that someone must have thought well of the fellow. But what sort of teacher a graduate instructor might prove to be is more often a matter of blind chance. At Stanford University, for example, the young graduate instructors inhabit a series of offices they call the Bull Pen. Some of these young men will be brilliant students who happen to have a natural talent for teaching; others will be serious students with no particular flair for expression; still others will be time-servers who have discovered the academic life a wonderful hideaway from the depressing reality that lies outside the academic world. In an age when anywhere from 70 to 90 per cent of graduates from some selective colleges, and up to 30 per cent of graduates from nonselective colleges, go on to graduate school, the case could be hardly otherwise—the percentages being large enough to assure a very mixed bag. The incoming freshman, presented with a schedule to fill out, knowing none of the available instructors by reputation and knowing nothing more about the courses, must take what he can when he can, and in the process, takes pot luck.

"The shape of many a kid's future life depends on which instructors he draws when he registers for classes," one Stanford professor said. "He might get some dodo who frosts him on the whole idea of going to college, or he might get some genius who really inspires him with purpose and desire."

"The graduate instructor," a Massachusetts Institute of Technology professor said, "is by no means the only chance a student takes."

Implying that professors may be just as poor teachers, if not worse, he said:

"It is a paradox, both here and elsewhere, that while so much money is being spent on research, practically none of it is spent in research on the learning process at the college level—and by the learning process I mean both the learning and the teaching. There's a kind of embarrassment at the college level in looking at teaching as though it were an art that really could be studied. We have some men on this faculty who have been teaching for years and who really do it rather poorly. For a good teacher, raising admissions standards means an opportunity to make his classes ever more interesting and exciting, but this means something quite different to the majority of college teachers who, frankly, aren't much good. To them, higher standards simply mean 'more of the same.' Their answer is, 'If yesterday we read ten novels a month, today we have smarter students so we will make them read thirty novels a month.' Two term papers become five. The result is that for the most part, college work is more difficult today than it was twenty-five years ago, not because the content of the courses has been qualitatively improved, but merely because more work is asked, with the result that most of it is simply dull. Not more interesting; just more work, and duller."

If teaching is an art, then of course it cannot be wholly learned. At some point, an artist needs talent, which is a gift from God. Technique, however, can make a craftsman, and techniques can certainly be learned. Unfortunately, few colleges pay sufficient attention to communicating intellectual excitement. The only matter of supreme importance is whether the teacher knows something about his subject. If a man has this, as duly certified by his academic degrees, and if he keeps on proving that he knows something by writing learned papers about it, he will have no trouble finding employment and promotion in the professorial ranks no matter how poorly he may communicate what he knows to the students in his classroom. Perhaps the most amazing of all things about college teaching is that no one presumes to judge the quality of the teacher's teaching—least of all, his fellow teachers. It is perhaps the only profession in which the performers are not held to some standards, even those of simple competence. The rule is, one professor must never go into another's classroom to sit in judgment on the man's competence as a teacher.

"The way it works at this place," one associate professor said, "the people in the department will ask the kids what they think of So-and-So, and the word gets around. Now, if you find a man whose classes are always jammed, you know he's popular, so you can say, 'He must be a good teacher.' If you have a man who never attracts more than five kids a semester, you can say, 'His course must be lousy,' and that he's terrible as a teacher. Or, you can look at it this way: If a man is popular, he must be giving a gut course, and you ought to get rid of him. If a man has only five students, you can say, 'Boy, he's really cracking down on them; he must be giving the toughest course in the school—we ought to promote him.'

"Most often," he said, "everybody knows who the really good students are—the kids who are obviously headed for graduate school—and *these* are the kids you ask about a man. If they say he's good, he's in; if they say he's bad, he's out. Or, you can say, 'If the grinds like him, maybe he isn't getting across to the

64

rest of the class.' After all, the really hot students who intend to go to grad school are pretty special kids. They're not going to be most of the class, but the teacher has to teach all of the class. Or, you can say, 'I hear it's only the grinds who don't like him, but those kids wouldn't like anybody.'

"What it comes down to is this," he concluded. "If you're a department head, and you either like the guy personally, or hate his guts, you have him coming or going. You can use whatever the kids say and pick whatever argument fits if you want to promote him or try to get rid of him."

Ability or inability to teach is seldom the basis on which a man is promoted or fired, however, as a recent example at Yale makes clear. Among Ivy League students, Yale enjoys the reputation of caring the most about good teaching and making the most determined efforts to see that professors—and not graduate instructors—are in the undergraduate classrooms. Yet in the fall of 1963, Yale decided not to promote an associate professor of English who was merely a good teacher. His sin of omission was that he had been so busy inspiring students that he had not published a learned paper or book in his field. The man was a victim of the notorius rule, *Publish or perish.*

"The only way you can tell what a man knows, is by what he publishes," a member of Yale's English department said of the case. "When you talk about a man's ability as a teacher, you must also ask whether what he teaches is *true.* Unless a man gives evidence of having kept up with current developments in his field, you cannot be sure that he has; you cannot be sure that what he is saying in class is still true. There was no question, from what the students said, that this man was, and is, a great teacher. There never was a question of firing him. There was a question about promoting him."

Promotion, he said, should be the reward of demonstrated scholarship.

Firing was the question, however, in the case of Tufts University vs. Dr. Woodrow Wilson Sayre in April, 1964. *The New York Times* reported that Tufts flatly told Dr. Sayre it was "satisfied that you have been effective in the classroom," but said it was letting Dr. Sayre go after seven years because "the promise of scholarly contribution has not materialized."

There are good arguments for Tufts' view. College professors are supposed to advance knowledge. Who else could? How can this be done except through scholarly research? What graduate school would attract scholars unless it could point to a faculty of agile minds, busily learning and reporting their discoveries? There is merit in the belief that a good teacher who does no research is not pulling his oar.

It is not the purpose of this book to try to resolve such arguments, but rather to observe and to report on the present climate. Throughout the land, the mood of the professor is arrogance. Long the butt of jokes and wretchedly paid, the professor now feels his hour has come. He daily becomes more valuable as college enrollment hugely increases at a far faster rate than teachers—good *or* bad—can be found. There is intense competition among colleges for good students and for foundation grants, both of which may be attracted only if the college can point to a faculty studded with prestigious professors. Wherefore, the colleges compete for the professors, and as *The New York Times* editorially said, emphasis on good teaching

66

vanishes in the process. For the professors know, *The New York Times* said, that a teacher's reward for brilliant teaching "is the gratitude of his limited number of students," but that the same energy put into research could produce a significant finding which "would result in fame, promotion, and lucrative consultantships." As one professor remarked, "the call to another institution has become a status symbol and everybody worries about who's been bid for." Thus the annual conclaves of learned professions become nothing more than public slave auctions, as one professor of English put it, "where you don't go to listen to the papers being delivered, but to talk with a guy who can hire you. You go there shyly to let it be known that your genius can be had for a couple more thousand a year."

Hence there is no longer a feeling of institutional loyalty on the part of the professors. As one said, "Everybody becomes a visiting professor and nobody can really keep an eye on the student's four-year stretch of education." To which it must be added that nobody much wants to, these days. The argument now is that the art of teaching is not of first importance at the college level, anyway.

"Teaching is relatively unimportant for the strongly motivated student whose loyalty is to the discipline and not to the faculty," one dean said. "The worst college teaching cannot entirely ruin Shakespeare. Our view is that the work is here for any student who wants to do the work, and that he is supposed to want to do it. If he has questions, we can answer him; we are not here to hold his hand."

"A teacher should not get too close to his students," a professor said. "Disciples are usually badly educated people. The real task is to wean the student away from the care of the teacher, not to keep the student tied to the teacher."

Still another professor said that it was unrealistic to demand that all college teachers be good teachers. He said "the number of saints in any profession is small. How many good plumbers are there among all plumbers? How many good lawyers? How many good businessmen, or politicians? Within any profession or trade, most of its practitioners will be relatively inept, and only a handful will be truly brilliant. Of course there are good teachers in any college, but relatively few. To expect anything else would be illogical."

The great question here is whether the colleges are not also being somewhat illogical if they believe that the incoming mass of students do not need teaching. It would seem that the present system of instruction and organization of courses is predicated on the notion that all who come to college are mature men and women who intend to go on to a graduate degree and make a career of scholarship. Perhaps these are the only people who *should* go to college, but the point is moot, because the fact is that half the high school population *does* go, and that nearly all incoming students are adolescents who still badly need guidance; whose intellectual interests are still largely plastic; who might be inspired to serious work if someone would take the pains to inspire them. Instead, the students arrive on campus to find themselves quickly hooked onto one sort of conveyor belt or another, ticketed for some narrow academic destination before they have time to decide whether that is where they want to go, or if the trip is necessary. Nearly all will complain of the teaching, both as to quality and kind, but their complaints about the teaching will be minor as compared to those they will make about their courses.

In an age of increasing specialization, the need for a general education was never more acute, nor so difficult to acquire. A question college students constantly ask is, "Where is this getting us?" By this, they mean, "Is this course relevant to anything I can use in the workaday world? If it is, I can't see it, and if it isn't, why study it?"

"Good teaching can provide relevance," the chairman of one English department said, "but the system does not produce good teachers, and, indeed, has scant room for them." It was his opinion that a student today must largely be his own teacher and work out his own theory of relativity.

A difficulty in seeing the woods for the trees is that college is increasingly becoming all trees and no woods. Few schools today preach the well-rounded man, and in those schools where production of the well-rounded man is still the purpose, that purpose is not always well-served. Briefly, today's courses tend toward narrower and narrower examination of particulars within specific fields; they tend to become related to nothing but the further study of themselves. Noticing this trend, a committee of senior professors at Harvard reported in May, 1964, that the American college is fast becoming "a hyphen between high school and graduate school." So it may be said that a crueler disappointment than Mickey Mouse, wretched teaching, and a sense of drift afflicts the intelligent, but as-yet-purposeless, boy who goes up to college expecting there to meet Mr. Chips who will help to mold him into the shape of a well-rounded man who knows a little about everything and a great deal about something. He will shortly find that the Renaissance is over, and Mr. Chips is dead, and that when today's courses are not Mickey Mouse, they are narrow preparations for graduate school.

4

Who is grading the graders?

Dr. Robert M. Hutchins believes the standards of our colleges "are undecipherable, their accomplishments dubious, their pretensions insufferable, their independence a sham, and their appeal to their constituency irrational and degrading."* Here is nothing new.

Throughout the history of institutional education, someone has been attacking the establishment along these lines—and not without justice. All universities have had to pander at times; to crawl before their constituencies. A state university lives at the mercy of its state legislature. Few private colleges are entirely out of the clutches of dead alumni or live trustees. But to the extent that universities are free to teach what they please, their standards, accomplishments, and pretensions are at least debatable. The central

* Addressing the January, 1964, meeting of the Association of American Colleges, as reported in *The New York Times.*

question, from the very beginning of organized education, has always been the relevance of the curriculum to reality. For example, Francis Bacon quit Cambridge when he discovered that what Cambridge thought was true, was probably false. In leaving, he seemed an intellectual heretic, for Cambridge was then regarded as the world's leading center of scientific thought.

It would seem that the value of any school may be measured by the extent to which it serves as a forum for the correction of its orthodox opinions. A school not in flux is dead, and one involved in self-examination is in a state of confusion. Either state can exasperate thoughtful, ignorant students who arrive on campus with the naïve belief that the courses they are about to take will add up to an education, or who in our age of specialization have been led to believe that there are always specific answers to specific questions, or some pat formula for each possible problem. If they attend a dead school, those who look will have no trouble discovering evidence of rigor mortis. They might then say with Philip Wylie that "Our universities would be better abolished, so as to be turned into something fresh and vital, than to be allowed to carry on in the revolting enterprise of stowing into every brain a few slices of science, a tenth of a language, a one-semester course of pedantic gibberish concerning obsolete philosophy, and the brittle prejudices of some young upstart in the nonexistent sciences of sociology and economics and, after that, informing the container of this uncongealed morass, via diploma, that he is 'educated.' "*

If the students come to a college that is in ferment, in which all values are challenged to the point where

* From his book *Generation of Vipers.*

people go about saying "truth is an employable illusion," then they might say, as one Harvard dropout did, "I want to get back to something basic—like carpentry."

The students' most common complaint is that relevance is missing in any case; that no one makes clear to them why they should study what they are asked to study. For example, a student who intends to major in business administration might wonder why he must read James Joyce, or take courses in comparative religion, the history of fine arts, biology, and Middle English poetry. So too, a student intent upon a literary career might be appalled by his requirements in behavioristic psychology. He might wonder why he must take the required course in mathematics.

"The professors don't know, themselves," one college boy said. "When you try to corner them on it, they can't explain. Finally they tell you the course is required."

Wherever such a professorial attitude exists, the typical result is that a student finds himself saddled with a roster of courses that somehow fails to impress him either as a specific vocational preparation or as a banquet for the hungry mind. One Yale boy put it thus:

"Gee, college is bad news. I have to do all this glop instead of doing what I want to do."

Another boy, registering as a freshman at a huge Midwestern state university, delightedly checked course after course in the university bulletin. Unfortunately, he had not read the bulletin carefully, for if he had, he would have known what his freshman guidance officer had to tell him.

"If you took all these courses, it would take you eight years to finish them and you wouldn't get a degree."

Patiently, the guidance officer explained that the boy could not take some of the courses he had checked until he had first taken certain other courses he hadn't checked. He pointed out that the boy's selection of courses—while no doubt comprising a splendid general education—did not include some of the courses required of candidates for the bachelor of arts degree.

"That's all right by me," the boy said. "Let's forget about the degree and just figure out how many of these courses I *can* take in four years."

"You can't do that. You are here as a candidate for the degree. You can't just take what you want, unless you are here as a special student."

"O.K., put me down as a special student."

"You cannot be a special student unless you are at least twenty-five years old and have permission from the registrar."

"I thought college was the place where you could study what you were interested in," the boy objected.

"People who have been over the ground before you have decided what it would be best for you to study at this time in your life. Now let's be serious about this. You will have to have English Comp. 1; that's basic. All freshmen take that. You will need one full course in natural science. How about geology?"

"How about biology instead?"

It turned out that the biology sections had been filled by the time this boy, whose last name began with letter R, was registering for his courses. A zoology section was still open, but it was offered on Monday, Wednesday, and Friday at 2 P.M.—the precise time at

74

which the mandatory course in English Comp. 1 was offered. Therefore zoology could not be fitted into the boy's schedule. Since he did not wish to undertake physics or chemistry, he was signed, sealed, and delivered to the freshman course in geology.

The remainder of his roster included a survey course in world history; one in the United States Constitution; another in geography. ("You'll find geography goes hand-in-hand with your geology.") He was not compelled to study a foreign language, for he was able to satisfy that degree requirement by passing the university examination on the basis of his high school French. He was signed to a one-hour course in romantic English poetry as an elective.

"You say you don't know what you want to do in life," his adviser said, "so let's proceed on the theory that you will major in English. If you do, then you will already have had one of the courses required for English majors."

The boy left the office looking somewhat dubiously at his schedule. None of these courses had been included in his original check list of subjects that had attracted him, but the English composition, history, and geology courses satisfied certain distribution requirements demanded of freshman candidates for the bachelor of arts degree. Vaguely depressed, he suspected that his schedule did not promise him a rousing life of the mind, and by midterm of his freshman year, he was quite sure it did not.

Perhaps a more poignant example is that of a Harvard sophomore who brought his study adviser a somewhat exotic list of courses in music, literature, and fine arts, including one in water-color technique. The boy was well aware of his strong natural talent for drawing, but this was not his primary reason for wanting to enroll in the course in water color. Rather, it was that the course was offered by an internationally famous artist who had but eight students. Here, at last, the boy thought, was an opportunity to take advantage of what Harvard ostensibly offers in its bulletin— personal instruction from a genius. The study adviser was unimpressed.

"If you take these courses," he said, tossing the list aside, "you'll get out of here with lots of style, but no content."

A question arises here as to the adviser's credentials as an adviser. He was not much older than the sophomore. He was a graduate student who had not attended Harvard as an undergraduate. He knew little more about Harvard's undergraduate courses than a second-term freshman. He had no training or experience in advising anyone on any matter under the sun. Still less had he an interest in human motivation, nor any personal interest in the hopes, aspirations, or individual capabilities of the young total strangers who came to him to have their college careers largely shaped by him. He was merely a young man whose entire adult life had been spent within the academic environment, and he happened to be intellectually arrogant enough to believe that painting with water colors was a waste of a college student's time. So he prescribed a schedule he believed to be more serious—one that led toward a graduate school.

In theory, a student is not bound to follow the adviser's advice. In practice, he almost always does, out of honest ignorance, or for fear of consequences, or a simple desire to please. So it was in this case. The following year, the student had left Cambridge forever, complaining that the courses he was asked to take were meaningless to him, and that he was wasting his time, and Harvard's time, and everyone's money, by remaining. Gone, too, was the distinguished artist, for reasons best known to Harvard and himself. Campus conjecture was that he left because there was almost no demand for his course. That is as may be. Perhaps there was a demand, systematically stamped out by young *idiots-savants* empowered to advise youngsters that college should be a cram shop for graduate school.

Harvard does have a tendency to provide an education that leads toward early specialization and graduate study. It is shared by every college of serious academic aspirations. Harvard worries about this. A Harvard faculty committee was established to look into the matter, and early in 1964 it reported that "it is repugnant in the extreme" to envision "a society of specialists" who are unaware of each other and of society at large, but that Harvard's undergraduate education—because of its tendency to become a specific preparation for graduate study—was contributing to the formation of just such a society. Their report was a plea for a return to the concept of the liberally educated man.

A professor at a small liberal arts college, noticing the trend toward early specialization at his school, argued the case from the student's point of view.

"Now look here," he said. "We preach the well-rounded man to a kid for his first seventeen or eighteen years, and then when he goes to college, we say 'get lopsided.' In this, perhaps society and the college are wrong.

"The whole matter usually becomes acute in sophomore year," he said, "because sophomore year is the

77

one in which most kids are asked to choose their majors. There is something slightly ridiculous about asking a nineteen-year-old to stake his life on the next ten minutes; to pick out some field in which to concentrate, graduate, and become immersed forever. For one thing, except for the very few kids who have been specialists since kindergarten—I'm thinking of the zoölogist of today who at age five was breeding white mice—most kids have no way of knowing what they'll want to do in the future; no way to pretest or otherwise sample careers. But we're offering everyone courses designed for the white-mice breeders. Of course, the kids could always go to some other college, but if they are bright enough to get in here, they might be insulted by what they were offered elsewhere.

"Sophomore year," he said reflectively, "is also the year when the kid who has been a bright freshman decides, 'I just can't do another paper.' He is tired of the lockstep. He's been doing a bang-up job of study for five years in a row, including the high school years, and he sees nothing ahead but three more of the same sort of years, and he is a tired soldier. He is particularly likely to blow up if he can't see where any of this is getting him."

The phrase "tired soldier" seemed exactly appropriate to one youngster who hurled a textbook across the sitting room of his Princeton suite.

"Christ," he said, "it isn't that I can't do this shit. I know I can do it. Anybody they let in here can do anything they offer. So why am I *not* doing it? It's because it's shit, shit, shit. I can't stand to read another Goddamned word of it, that's why. I won't read it and I won't go to that stupid, stupid class, and that's why I'm flunking it. It's why I'll probably flunk right on out of here. Just a minute—listen to this."

He lunged out of his chair, picked up the book, opened the pages at random, and read a paragraph of viscous mumbo-jumbo some forty-eight lines long that a more skillful author might have been able to put into a few lines of simple English.

Too much should not be made of the youngster's argument, for he had no option but to do the work, or fail. There are many occasions in life when one must undertake detestable drudgery, and it is well for youth to begin to understand this proposition. Further, the fact that the boy found the course infuriating did not necessarily mean that the content of the course was not important for him to understand, or that the discipline required to understand it could not be brought to bear on other matters in the workaday world. On the other hand, it was perfectly true that he found the course exasperatingly dull, and at least one of its texts so badly written as to be virtually unreadable. Perhaps the instructor was partially at fault for not making the subject matter more comprehensible and pertinent, or for not being alert to the fact that at least one of his students needed some sort of help. As we shall see in the next chapters, the boy's real problem may have been an emotional one. For whatever combination of reasons, the ultimate fact was that a bright boy had worked himself into a profane, puerile rage bordering on hysteria. In such a state, it was impossible for him to do effective work in this, or any other course. When he resigned from the college before being asked to leave, one of his professors merely shrugged.

"What was the point of his staying here, paying out a large sum for tuition, paying for room and board, when nothing was happening for him?" the professor asked. "When nothing was effective? Why not pull

79

out now and go get a job? Why not spend the time profitably, not spend some money, but earn some?"

The professor's blithe view of a student's leaving Princeton at a time when the whole world apparently believes that a college education is a *sine qua non* might strike some people as verging on the incomprehensible. College authorities, however, generally take a calmer view of a student's leaving than does the student, or society at large. Perhaps it is because they know better than anyone else that college is not for everyone, no matter how bright, and that a prescribed course of studies may often stand between a particular boy and his acquiring the kind of education that would be beneficial to him.

"When students read of fighting in Viet Nam, and troubles in Algiers, or in South Philadelphia or in Harlem, they wonder what they are doing here," one University of Pennsylvania professor said. "I am reminded of a time during the Second World War when I was working in the library and a colleague of mine was busy across the table from me, surrounded by a pile of books, annotating an Icelandic saga. He looked up and said, 'Silly, isn't it?' He needed to say no more. With the whole world in flames and the best of our students gone to war, there we were, two moles digging in the dust of dead centuries.

"By the way," he said, "do moles dig in dust? I'm not at all certain that they do."

"Society," another professor said, "thinks there is some magic in four years with a diploma. It would be a step in the right direction if the public were to understand the more subtle meanings of an education; that it isn't related, one-to-one, to a set of courses culminating in a degree."

"Just because a boy has the brains for a degree," a dean of students said, "this is no reason why he ought to gun for one. For some students, college just gets in the way. We had one brilliant boy who left us to go to Hollywood to take a job as a cameraman. Today he is a producer. Although we might not like to think so, because we think what we do is valuable, maybe that fellow is better off for not having wasted another year here."

"He was the kind of student who identified so powerfully with the kind of intellectual life here that he had a certain kind of disdain for the time-serving, marching-along-through-courses aspect of it," an associate in the dean's office explained. "He was the kind who felt that a more genuine expression of his interest could come through reading. Many students believe this, but it works only for the very few who can actually discipline themselves to do the reading. He was one of the few."

At hazard, it would seem that the violence with which a student reacts against his courses is directly proportional to the social pressure put on him to regard college as Paradise despite the fact that he has come to think of it as Limbo. The rule is, the more prestigious the college and the brighter the students, the greater the demand that the students love the college, and the more violent the expressions of disenchantment in the event this love affair is broken off. The Princeton boy's hysterical reaction may be contrasted with the muted tones of disappointment to be heard at another kind of school.

For example, disenchantment over the course offerings is quite general at one low-powered city university that caters principally to students of modest ability who for the most part are the first members of their families ever to attend a college. But few of these terribly serious, vocationally oriented students allow their dissatisfactions to carry them to the point of actually quitting school. The issues are stark to them: A college degree is a badge of success, a sure passport to better-paying jobs than their fathers hold.

At this university, situated in a slum, the pursuit of learning proceeds in bitter earnest. Looking in on a classroom chosen at random, we find it occupied by twenty-one freshmen who have survived the holocaust of the midyear examination that flushed a majority of their classmates out of formal education forever. No less than seventeen of these twenty-one survivors expect the school to prepare them narrowly for specific vocations. Seven intend to become dentists; five would be teachers; one a doctor; one a hospital administrator; another a social worker; one an athletic coach; and one a writer. The remaining four have not yet decided upon future careers. They say they are in college to acquire a general education, and they happen to have the highest average grades among the twenty-one students. Interestingly enough, three of these four say they hope to transfer to better universities next year. Only one third of the twenty-one students believe that this city university deserves a high academic rating. None believe that it ranks with the best. Nearly half are satisfied with their lot, resigned to the fact—or to what they believe to be the fact—that they are mediocre people. National test scores have assured them that this is the case insofar as academic aptitude and achievement are concerned. The average reading level of the class is that of the tenth grade, according to a national standard test. Perhaps their sense of relative inferiority (which is very real, if possibly unwarranted) contributes to the observable bitterness with which they discuss their college work. While their college grades average one whole mark lower than their high school grade averages, most of these students say they do not find the college work to be as difficult as they had anticipated, and they say that much of it is a rehash of knowledge already acquired in high school. What they say may not necessarily be true, but it is a fact that they believe it to be true, and hence they feel that, in some way, they have been cheated.

"This is just the thirteenth grade of the city public school system," one girl said. "So this is college?"

Asked whether they felt their courses were directly or indirectly related to their purposes for being in college, two thirds of them said No. The most charitable majority view was that of the boy who said he intended to become a medical doctor.

"My courses are not directly aimed at that goal," he said. "But indirectly they are helping me toward it. I find things I have learned in anthropology, German, and sociology do come up and aid me in other more directly relevant subjects like chemistry."

Other students answered the question as follows:

"Definitely not—a French teacher has no need for a math course."

"I am disillusioned by the impersonality of the students and teachers."

"History is worthless to a dentist."

"This is a sheepskin factory to help people obtain a job. I came here involuntarily, and I have not found many fellow students trying to educate themselves for their own self-gratification, but instead for socioeconomic reasons."

"Every student is just an IBM number."

"God, no. I'll be the only hospital administrator with a Spanish accent and a fluent account of wars fought 300 years ago."

"Some classes I hate. They don't apply to my profession as a teacher."

"I feel some liberal arts courses are a waste of time."

"I'm going to college to learn whatever I can in the fields that interest me, and I'll have to expect courses that don't mean a thing to me."

"I see no reason why an elementary education teacher needs to know about statistics and other such subjects."

"Some of the students know more than the teachers. A senior student is teaching one class. The instructors can't teach."

"Very few courses are related, and in a very minor way, if at all."

If it is true that most college students are in some way dissatisfied with at least some of the courses they are required to take, it is also true that this dissastisfaction is relatively minor. However general, it is usually no more exasperating than a low-grade toothache that comes at random moments. After all, most students have no idea as to what courses of study might constitute an education. Even those who attend in order to acquire specific vocational skills are in no position to say whether the courses put before them will, or will not, serve the end in view. There is much they must all take on faith, and most students accept what they are given without much complaint. The major source of irritation is not just that a course may seem irrelevant and immaterial. It is that they are graded in competition with one another in an activity which they might regard as not worth doing well.

"I do wish," said Robert Iffert, "that we could do away with all this fol-de-rol of grading and compulsory attendance-record-keeping that we have fallen into because of administrative convenience. This is not the way people out in the world are rated. It is artificial insofar as predicting anything that is going to happen is concerned. There are plenty of people who failed college who, in the genuine competition, have done pretty well."

The trouble is, no school has yet devised a marking system satisfactory to everyone, but what is perhaps worse, there are no clearly defined national standards whereby collegiate academic performance can be measured. (Much less can academic performance in college, no matter how graded, be considered an unfailing determinant, or predictor, of future performance in the nonacademic tasks of the workaday world.)

For example, it is fairly easy to assign grade values for work done in reading, writing, and arithmetic at the primitive level of elementary school. We can establish national standards of achievement in these skills. It is much more difficult at the high school level to measure the quality of work done, and to project this measurement on a national scale. How, for instance, can anyone really determine that Willie's eleventh-grade perceptions of *Moby Dick* are worth 89 points, while those of his classmate, Jane, are worth 61½? Next, how can you compare the aesthetic sensibilities of Jane and Willie with those of children in another high school where a course in *Moby Dick* is not offered, but where the children are required to read *Ivanhoe* instead? At the college level, chaos prevails. Each college has a right to say that it will grant its degree only to those students who earn what the college believes to be passing grades in the work offered at that college. So the graduate of one university cannot be regarded as the equal of the graduates of all others. And within any college, the marking system may seem unfair to the students. For instance, Harvard draws its students from within the upper 2 per cent of the nation's most intelligent youth. But then, as the master of one of Harvard's houses explained, "The professor has general control over the section men [graduate instructors] working under him and supervises their grading to see that it does not violate the predicted curve. This means they have to make the curve come out evenly—not that the instructors have any special reference to any special student, nor that they consider the learning process to be a communication from one person to another person. A real question for Harvard is how to keep up the confidence and drive of the lower half of Harvard's classes, which by any national standard would entirely consist of most remarkably superior students."

The curve to which he referred may be explained as follows:

In any group of students studying a particular subject, the performance of a few will be relatively excellent. A few will seem to be relative failures, and the performance of most will appear to be relatively mediocre. If their different performances were to be given numerical values, and if these values were then plotted as points on a graph and a line were drawn connecting all the points, the shape of the line would be predictable. It would be a bell-shaped curve—the so-called normal curve. If grade values were to be assigned on the basis of this curve, then a few students would receive A's; some, Bs; the majority, Cs; some, Ds; and a few would fail.

Thus one boy who scored 96 out of a possible 100 on one Harvard French examination was horrified to find this mark worth a C— when the numerical scores of his classmates were used to form a curve. It is conceivable that a boy who scored 80 on that particular examination at Harvard would have failed—by Harvard's terms. It is also quite possible that if the same examination had been administered to students at X College, the brightest X College French scholar might have attained no more than a 20 on Harvard's scale. So one question is: Is it a service to the nation to collect into a few schools a student body consisting entirely of the nation's most able youngsters and then predict relative failure there for some of them, when by any conceivable national criteria, the worst of them would seem distinctly superior in ability and achievement to 98 per cent of all the rest of the nation's college students? Another question is: Is it any real service to the carefully selected students at a rigorous college to pit them in a battle of survival against each other?

The Harvard house master thought the answer to both questions was No.

"Our biggest problem," he said, "is this marking on the curve, since the selection is already so damned good."

"I couldn't agree with you more," a Massachusetts Institute of Technology colleague told him. "And *this* is why so many of *our* professors don't mark on the curve, although it could be said the whole college lives on a national curve."

"Normal curves should hardly apply to honors students, or perhaps, to any of our undergraduates," a University of Pennsylvania professor suggested. "And how to grade their work for admission to graduate school is a frightful headache to us. But more important, you can imagine the pressure on the students who know that the only safe, sure path to graduate school is good grades. You are really demanding that each of the best try to be better than all the rest of the best, in every subject, like it or not, which, of course, is an impossible situation."

"At this school," a professor at another college said, "we look at an incoming freshman's aptitude and achievement test scores, compare them with those of the rest of the people who will be his classmates, and then predict what grades he will earn here. Now, when we do this, aren't we really saying, 'We will do nothing for you here?' If we are, then I am tempted to suggest that we might as well run an applicant's test scores through an IBM machine that would give him his grades, and grind out a diploma which we could mail to him upon receipt of his check covering four years' tuition, and save him all the bother of actually coming here."

If the professors seem somewhat at a loss to arrive at an equable marking system, the students are at no loss of words to say what they think of the notion that intellectual efforts can always be ascribed relative values.

"What *I* want to know is what *is* failure, anyway?" a student demanded. "I have a guy teaching me that *I* think is a failure. He doesn't like my idea of his course, and I don't like his. Who is to say which of us is right? As it turns out, he has the power to flunk me, but I don't have the power to flunk him. A lot of this is personality clash, but apart from that stuff, let's look at the course. I think I've got something out of it, and he doesn't think I have. As far as I'm concerned, the *course* isn't a failure. I know I've learned something from it. What I've learned satisfies my curiosity in it, and what else do you want? I didn't come here to take it, but I took it when they gave it to me, and I think I understand it as well as anybody else in the class. The only reason I may flunk it is because of this personality difference and because I don't—and won't

see it his way. If I told him I saw it his way, I'd pass in a breeze, but then I'd be dishonest. If you have an honest disagreement, does this mean you're a failure? Let's look at it this way: Don't you have to know more about something to *disagree* with it than you have to know to go along with it?"

The answer to the boy's question varies between "yes, sometimes" and "perhaps." It is of such questions that colleges are made. And of such answers.

Generally speaking, most students do not allow their dissatisfactions with their courses or with the marking systems to get the better of them. Those who drop out will not always cite these dissatisfactions as the *major* reasons for their leaving. A study of dropouts at one college disclosed that 61 per cent of them said they were satisfied by their relatively brief sojourns on campus. They said they felt they had got out of the college all they had wanted to get out of it. Their view seemed charitable. It was not that the courses were bad, nor that the college was bad, but rather that the courses meant nothing much one way or another to *them*, and that however good the college might be for some people, it was not where *they* wanted to be.

It is nevertheless a fact that some will leave precisely because of their disappointment with course offerings. Usually, however, this will be listed as one item in a long catalogue of a student's reasons for withdrawal. It may be a rationalization, but it is nearly always mentioned—if only to be ascribed as a purely personal, and not necessarily universally valid, complaint. The students who remain to be graduated are also likely to say that not all of the work they were asked to do meant much in particular to them and that the marking system was not connected to any rational process of judgment.

5

Why sophomores slump

Nothing is more disturbing to college authorities than
the phenomenon they call sophomore slump. The
students who suffer from it are not those who flunk
out because the work is beyond them. Rather, they
are bright students who could do the work, but who,
for reasons best known to their psychiatrists, are not
doing it. Their number also includes those students
who *are* doing the work, often earning honor grades,
but who decide that the work is not worth doing and
pack their bags and leave. A common presumption is
that if a successful student leaves college, he must
have something wrong with him.

Reporting on the increasing incidence of sophomore slump, a Columbia University alumni quarterly
in April, 1964, called attention "to the new problem
of students' problems." In the same month *The
New York Times* said that increasing numbers of

91

students at prestige colleges, who had moved heaven and earth to get in, are now pleading to get out—despite creditable academic performance. The reason why this plea is characteristically uttered during sophomore year has nothing to do with the nature of second-year work. Most of those who walk out do so in sophomore year. They will have found reasons for leaving when they were freshmen but will have been badgered by their parents, or by their own consciences, to try to stick it out for another year before undertaking an action that nearly everyone would think unwise. Caught between their intuitive knowledge that college is no place for them and everyone else's opinion that college is the only right place for them, many students become mentally ill. The early symptoms of sophomore slump range from apathy to hysteria. Neurodermatitis, a psychosomatic skin rash, is common in selective colleges. The boy who commits suicide is rare, but less rare is the one who attempts suicide—or (perhaps more properly) pretends to attempt to commit suicide. At Yale, at least one boy comes down with a high fever at every examination period and runs off to the infirmary to hide. At Cornell, one student behaved in a manner that suggested something was troubling him. He ran amuck in the dormitory.

"College students are crowding the deans' lists and the psychiatrists' couches," Fred M. Hechinger, education editor of *The New York Times* wrote. "Each year admissions officers report incoming students to be intellectually superior to the previous year's entries. But each year, too, campus observers say that these same students are plagued by increasingly serious emotional problems. A Harvard psychiatrist warned that the traditional gap between intellectual and emotional maturity in late adolescence is getting wider. He added that 'many of the most exceptional students are among the most immature.'"

Mr. Hechinger went on to report that at Columbia, the number of students seeking psychiatric help has tripled in the last decade; that Yale employs eleven full-time and nine part-time professional workers in its mental hygiene clinic; that Harvard's facilities are so widely used that some students refer to the Health Service, directed by Dr. Dana L. Farnsworth, as "the Farnsworth-Hilton."

Perhaps the noticeable increase in the number of students receiving psychiatric therapy during the last decade merely reflects both the increase in the total number of students and in the availability of mental health services and is not a *proportional* increase in mental illness. But whether the matter reflects whole numbers or a ratio is somewhat beside the point. What *does* seem significant is that psychiatrists both on campus and in private practice agree with college deans that the problem is essentially one of emotional immaturity. They are saying that an emotionally immature student tends to come apart under college stress. To which the deans quickly add that if a student jumps the tracks this is none of the college's doing. One University of Pennsylvania admissions officer expressed the majority view of his colleagues thus:

"Of those who dropped out, a number had availed themselves of the psychiatric agency or of the counseling service, and an analysis of these cases indicates they had emotional problems before they came to the university. These for the most part were minor personality disorders that interfered with the student's doing good work; they resulted from unresolved family problems, or personal emotional problems. In most cases, the students brought these with them to college."

"To give you an example," said the dean of men at one highly selective coeducational college, "I can think of one who was a freshman here last year who did very poor work in his first term, but who was good enough to stay into the second term, but it looked like a thoroughly hopeless proposition because the fellow was responding to us with a kind of massive passivity. He just wasn't getting anything done. He made me think of the fellow in the eight-oared shell who gets confused, tired, and who simply pulls his oar in and rides the rest of the way. Now, we have fairly competent counseling resources here. This lad saw one of our psychiatrists for quite a number of sessions. That didn't help him. Now, my hunch is, this fellow's passivity grew out of his total past experience. His father had been killed in the war. He had grown up in a small town and apparently without any significant close male influence. I think he had simply not been accumulating, over the years, those small but unobtrusive bits of experience that would have given him the emotional strength to deal with the demands that he had to face here. This passivity had never shown up in high school, because he was bright, and there the absence of this kind of otherwise normal growth had never revealed itself. So he was not a mistake by the admissions office, to my mind. Rather few high schools really are challenging. Especially when you take a boy who may be really bright and who doesn't realize the extent to which he is doing good work at only a fraction of the energy and determination that he should be using. So he wasn't getting anything done. He wasn't even going to class. Finally, he saw that there was just no point in going on."

Before we accept the deans' assurances that the students bring their problems with them and the psychiatrists' argument that the problem is essentially one of emotional immaturity, some further questions seem in order. After all, the youngsters we send off to places like Harvard, Yale, and Columbia are orderly, extremely bright boys of outstanding character and attainments. They would be unacceptable to these colleges if they were not. If the colleges then return some of these same young people to us as psychiatric patients two years later, are we not entitled to suspect that their present mental condition might somehow be connected to something that happened to them in college?

By what standards do the college psychiatrists judge them to be immature? A psychiatrist is prone to measure maturity by the degree to which an individual adapts or adjusts to, or accepts or makes his peace with, the social milieu in which he finds himself. The psychiatrist is not prone to look with favor upon the man who suggests that everyone is out of step but him, or upon the man whose reaction to society is to reject it. But come now: Is the student who loves his courses, or the one who at least obediently swallows them, always to be considered emotionally mature? If such were the collegiate view, would it not be a self-serving one? Is such a student necessarily less infantile than the one who detests the work set before him, who loathes everything about the college and says so? Is it not quite possible that a youngster may—after mature deliberation—decide that college is no place for him *and then become emotionally overwrought in the course of acting on his decision to leave?*

For example, here is Gregory, an Ivy League sophomore. He has no specific vocational interest as yet, but is being pushed into an English major he does not want, because he must select a major in his sophomore year. He is being pushed into English because that department seems to be the catchall for the undecided. His feeling of nondirection is exacerbated when he sees the purposeful industry of so many of his classmates, more than half of whom are brighter than he. He is disappointed in himself for not doing as well as he knows he could. He made the dean's list as a freshman, but now, having a general distaste for certain required subjects, and failing to see what these courses might mean to him, he cannot (or at least does not) put forth the same effort he did as a freshman. He feels that some of his low grades are entirely undeserved and that some of his teachers are not worthy of respect. He cannot see how college is really connected to himself and to his general interest in the creative arts. While he feels that he will some day do "something creative," and most probably something involving writing, he suspects that to major in English is not always the best way to prepare for a literary career. For example, he finds that the creative writing course he is taking has apparently been designed to curb literary experimentation rather than to encourage it. He is fond of quoting the Harvard president who said, "Whenever we find a spark of genius, we water it." In two years, he has made but two friends. In high school, he had been extremely popular and had dated steadily. He has broken up with his high school girl and has not yet found another. He is worried because he has so few friends at college but does not think this is his fault. He says it is because "all the guys around here are wrapped up in themselves. There are two thousand bright kids here, and not one good guy in the bunch." All in all, he is no longer the healthy, happy, popular boy who came to the college as a freshman but has become moody, somewhat withdrawn, and wants very badly to leave.

Arrayed against Gregory's desire to leave is his certain knowledge that his doing so would dismay his parents and disappoint his former high school teachers; his lonely fear that none of them will understand; his share of the common belief that it is difficult to make one's way in the world without a college diploma; his fear that if he quits college, he may forfeit his chance to marry a college girl. All this, and more, is placed in the scale against his absolute knowledge that he positively detests his present situation. If he works himself into a case of academic combat fatigue in the course of screwing up his courage to act upon his knowledge, and leave, are we to say he lacked emotional maturity? Can we not suggest that he simply lacked experience in acting as the field commander of himself? That his strategy was mature enough, but his tactics were deplorable? For instance, we might agree that it would be sound strategy for Gregory to extricate himself from a bad situation, but suggest that a wiser tactic than quitting, cold turkey, would be to switch majors or transfer to another college. But to switch majors, or transfer, calls for intellectual decision on a basis of sound information. It has nothing to do with the emotions.

It would seem that the occasional professor who actually takes an interest in his students as people is often a more charitable judge of the situation than are the deans and the psychiatrists.

"When a student gets into his sophomore year," one such professor said, "he begins to question at the same time he has now broken away from his home and parents to become a person. He begins to question the whole of his life and the things he has pursued, and has given such a tremendous amount of his energies to.

"The students," he continued, "will claim they have girl worries. They will say, 'My girl won't sleep with me.' They have war worries: 'We're just going to have to go into the Army and be killed in some damned rice paddy.' And they say they want to take a year off 'to enjoy life while we still can.' But these are not the real reasons why they are not doing well. The real reasons are found when the conversations in the dormitories shift to 'What does it all mean?' and 'What's the use of it all?' and 'Why am I here?'

"A problem arises when you assemble on one campus nothing but students who have been measured a dozen different ways and have been found superior in each of them. Their records in their prior milieus showed solid achievement, even brilliance, and certainly great promise. They are obviously expected to do as well relatively in life in the future as they have to date—to be among the upper one per cent of the adult, effective citizenry. So. Now we have them all at one school and mark them on the basis of their competition with one another—not, as before or in future, on the basis of how well they do as compared with the other 99 per cent of the population. We mark on the curve, flunking some out and giving most of them C. Where is this getting them, the college, or any of us? *This* is what contributes to the stress that

98

most strongly shows up in sophomore year, and this is what is behind those questions, 'What does this mean?' and 'What am I doing in this place?'

"When they look outside the college walls, they see policemen setting dogs on Negroes, a society full of wars and jails, in which the greatest rewards are reserved for those who manufacture, advertise, and market mass-produced junk and physical ugliness; and some of them reject it. If you are to tell them they will need a college degree in order to compete in this sick world, they will reject the college degree or they will go to the other extreme of going on to graduate school in order to stay in the academic womb forever. In either event, such students could be called dropouts, but it is not college they are dropping out of; they are dropping out of the world; and it is my belief that only our most brilliant students do this and that the whole system is really geared for the mediocre."

Another view was held by one of the professor's colleagues, who said:

"In reality, the process of selection here is to admit only those students who are most likely to drop out when we search out those who show evidence of thinking for themselves and who are given to acting for themselves. Here is the student who is the potential poet, painter, or writer; the one who wants to work on independent projects. Then he runs into professors who are dull, and classes that are dull. You never know around here whether a bright boy is going to spend his senior year writing a thesis or spend the next six years roaming around the world instead. These are the people who want to prove themselves. They have a real need for a real challenge, but for at least sixteen years, school and college offer them nothing but aca-

99

demic challenges which they grow tired of meeting. Each year we lose students of great promise who are tired of proving over and over again that they can do academic work, but who now badly need to prove to themselves that they can survive on their own in the outside world without knuckling under or accepting, necessarily, that world's values."

"For some people, sophomore slump is just a means of attracting attention," a psychologist at a women's college said. "A girl comes here from a warm, loving home where everyone worshiped her. She comes from a school where she was the honor student and a valuable member of the student council, and where, perhaps, she was also socially successful. Then she comes here where the work is more difficult than any she has done before, where the teachers seem cold and aloof and the other girls all seem to be interested in nothing but work, where she has no friends; and an incredible loneliness closes in. No one notices her. Her best work may be quite good, but so is everyone else's, and she finds her name missing, for the first time in her life, from the honor roll. She is desperately unhappy, but she remembers the sacrifices her family made to send her here and feels she must make a go of it somehow. Worry about making a go of it may, however, result in a lower quality of her work, with resultant lower grades. If on top of all this, she sees her classmates leaving the campus for week ends at Yale when nobody is asking her for a date, she will begin to think she is unattractive to men and a failure as a woman as well as a failure as a student."

In such a plight, the psychologist said, a girl may make a public show of not working, of smoking and drinking too much, of pretending that she is not a virgin—all in order to attract someone's attention. The predictable result of this footless activity is that her grades will slip to the point where the dean's office will express its interest in her by putting her on probation or by asking her to leave. Or, in her lonely depression, the girl may become pregnant, the psychologist said. His findings agreed with those of social workers who say that most girls who become pregnant out of wedlock are *not* the victims of ignorance or accident. Such pregnancy, he said, is almost always the girl's deliberate, if subconscious, choice: it is her way of seeking to revenge herself upon her parents, or upon her college, or upon society in general.

"It is her way of saying," he said, "I'll fix *you*. I'll show you who *I* am."

A far more typical example of sophomore slump will be seen in a letter one girl wrote to a friend:

"I arrived at Smith excited; elated at leaving home and breaking the old strings back into the past; feeling that the whole world of knowledge was open to me and I could strive and gain.

"By Christmas vacation I wanted to leave so badly I could have screamed. I was, and still am, fed up with the entire environment both academic and beyond. I wanted to learn, and to carry my thoughts beyond the classroom and apply them to myself and the world. I wanted to talk with my friends about books and ideas. But the only discussions were about hairdos, clothes and boys, getting snowed and falling in love. Everyone seemed empty, void of interest in ideas beyond what mark they were given for learning them. I didn't stop trying to find a communion of minds. I carried it into the social system. This was even worse. The dating system, in which girls feel like animals set up on an auction block and bid on, cannot result in any good communication. No boy wants to talk to a girl he's out with, because he doesn't actually feel she is a human being, but merely a plaything to dance with and drink with.

"In back of this stop sign for ideas at the door of the classroom is the amount of work everyone is forced to do. There is no time to think because no one can stop working for one minute or they would be behind. And if you want to waste some time you don't sit down and discuss books and ideas because that is too close to the academic. And when the week end comes, you drop the whole front and go out and get plowed and feel very satisfied because you escaped.

"The need for escaping becomes basic. You go off to as many men's colleges for week ends as is possible. You refuse to sit at college any week end without a date. But the week ends away don't help because it's the same split work-play atmosphere with the same type of people and the dates help even less.

"The problem comes down to the fact that a college throws together people who range in age from seventeen to twenty-two and places them in an academic atmosphere, but almost entirely out of contact with other ages. You are forced to be your own God and to decide the problems of life in an atmosphere that provides no perspective. You feel typed wherever you go. In the small town where you reside, you cannot get away from being a 'Smithie.' You cannot lose your false identity and you find it increasingly hard to find a self-made identity.

"You dream of the city, the place where you can do what you want in your own way and face everyone on equal territory without a sign around your neck, saying, 'I am a Smith girl,' because no one will know who you are or care beyond the identity of the person facing them.

"I have recently felt that if I'm going to have to endure four years of college, I might as well have an easy means of escaping the falsity and emptiness that pervades most aspects of campus life. I want a city to roam in, people to talk to who have no interest in me, who will not type me. I want to enter into the coldness that people live in for the rest of their lives.

"First we are in the warm comfortable womb of our mothers and then we enter the world with that first piercing scream. We go to kindergarten and grade school and are protected from evil and sin. We learn more and grow and go to high school and feel some of the coldness, the winter, the 'heart of darkness,' but we can still come home. We can still have the warmth and comfort of parents and teachers and friends who know us for ourselves.

"We leave for college and we have no home any more. No one really cares about us. We get new friends to ward off the blow of cold air, but it still hurts. And yet I and many others find that the ways in which college tries to make amends won't work. We want to face the coldness, at least for part of the time, in a crowd which doesn't know us and doesn't care. We want to face a reality that cannot be found on a closed-off campus and on many other campuses of men's colleges having a wild week end to make up for the terrific amount of work. We want to live."

The young lady's letter suggests that if emotional conflicts erupt in college, one explanation could be that the collegiate world is a peculiar one and that students are plunged into it without the slightest preparation for what to expect. This immersion occurs during the very years in which the greatest personality changes take place; precisely at the time when maturing young-sters feel most betwixt and between. One can well imagine that the boy who leaves a remote Idaho vil-lage to enter a sophisticated, high-powered Ivy League college might find the academic work the least of his problems. Again, if, coming from a township of some 500 souls, he were to enter a huge state university that had 20,000 undergraduates on campus, he might drown of loneliness in a sea of people. If he should, are we to say that he was emotionally immature? Or that he lacked information and experience?

A somewhat more common type of undergraduate than the highly intelligent Smith girl or the boy from the provinces would be the youngster of no particular talent who comes from a metropolitan area where he had been educated in some undemanding, permissive suburban public school system; raised in a youth-oriented society that glitters with sexual fantasies and which incessantly advertises that life can be fun with no down payment required. Car-pooled from his box-like home to the Cub Scouts and then to the Little League and the dancing class; encouraged to begin dating in a junior high school that boasts a football team complete with thirteen-year-old drum majorettes and beauty queens; given a car of his own to drive to a high school that offers a course in preparation for mar-riage, complete with mock weddings and mock recep-tions—such a candidate for a bachelor's degree has had his hand held and his nose wiped at every stage of the way. He has been the center of everyone's atten-tion—not merely that of his doting parents who in a hundred ways make his life vicariously their own. He has also been brought up to believe that fun is, essentially, an activity that can occur only somewhere other than at home—that if you want to have fun, you must get into an automobile and drive to where the fun can be had. To be sure, he has been subjected to great pressure to do well in his studies in order that he may win admission to a good college, but college has been held out to him as a place where more fun is to be had, and as the necessary gateway to the advertised American Dream. His high school studies will not have been demanding, but if the pressure to earn good grades in them has at times seemed too much for him, his parents may have given him tranquilizers.

"I am sure parents are giving them tranquilizers to help them avoid cracking under the pressure for good grades," said a New Jersey Health Department physician, assigned to find out why increasing numbers of grade-school children were arriving in school in states of foggy euphoria. "I have found out from fellow pediatricians that parents are slipping the children sedatives, too. They tell me it is quite common."

The doctor added that he was certain that the pressure to earn good grades was engendered by the ever-keener competition for admission to college and that this entire situation was "fomented by overanxious parents and schools."

A question might be asked as to who has the emotional problem: the society or its children? But let us return to the college campus.

A tranquilized child, pap-fed on the fun-dream, could find the collegiate experience appalling. All at once, he would be thrust into a world in which few adults would take an interest in him. College would prove not to be fun, but as the students say, "a real drag." The college authorities would not let him have his automobile, so he could not dash away to wherever fun allegedly happens. No one would give him tranquilizers any more. If he wanted them, he would have to go to the drugstore all by himself, and if he took the pills, his work would suffer, and if he didn't do the work, Pfft! would go his supposed chance of being able to acquire the advertised good things of the American Dream—the remunerative job, the fun-making Cadillac, the house in the good residential area, the back-yard swimming pool, the speedboat, the country-club membership.

To be sure, most of the students who have been brought up with a banal suburban sense of values can do well enough in some college. Everyone admitted to a selective college is basically intelligent enough to skate through on Cs and Ds if he makes *some* effort. The question is whether he can make the effort; whether he can quickly adapt to radically different circumstances and ways of looking at things. A somewhat childish student can do so fairly easily, learning just enough from his courses to pass them, but without examining them to ask what they might mean to him apart from their contribution to his degree requirements. Meanwhile, he can satisfy his need for fun by joining a fraternity, gulping goldfish, engaging in competitions to see how many students can jam themselves into a phone booth, or how swiftly he can demolish an old piano with an ax or push a double bed down a highway, or he can go hooting off to the girls' dormitory to steal a pair of panties. Such a lad will quite probably remain to be graduated, move smoothly into a corporate job, and remain a bright, fun-loving boy and a bore forever. Our alumni societies are full of them. But, for a more perceptive student, the difference between a liberal arts college's sense of values and his suburban sense of values, borne in upon him as subtly as a kick in the face and at the most wakeful moment of his life, demands what John Foster Dulles called an agonizing reappraisal.

Briefly, the most prestigious liberal arts colleges sing the virtues of the inquiring mind and the examined life, while society chiefly rewards the accepting, conforming man. Characteristically, those young people whom the liberal arts professors regard as their best students have nothing but scorn for the business man and all his works. The question here is not so much whether the good professors are in touch with reality, as whether they *should* be, and many a newly awakened student will have considerable difficulty trying to sort out the answer for himself.

Conscious of his emergent self and of the necessity for personal choice, many a sophomore echoes the boy who said:

"You tell me I have to have a degree to get a job, and I say to you that I don't want your lousy job. And what do you say to that? If there's one thing I'm *not* going to do, it's spend my life going to work from nine to five in some office for some large corporation that sells some junk nobody needs. Sure, they give you money for it, like a carrot on a stick in front of the nose of a rabbit on a treadmill. Every once in a while, they let you eat some of the carrot so you can get back on the treadmill and run faster. All right, if that's the way the world goes round, you can have it—but I'm not going to have anything to do with it."

It serves no purpose to tell such a student that he must be immature or that he has an emotional problem. Nor is it always a good answer to try to adjust him to a society that may well be more disturbed than he. It would seem wiser to agree with him, to say, "You may be perfectly right. Now what *do* you want to do instead, and is there anything we can do to help?" Such an answer might get matters off dead center, but unfortunately we most generally attempt to push a slumping sophomore back into line instead of allowing him freedom to blaze a trail for himself.

"The university tries to have people, what you might say, spotters, around campus who become aware of the student's difficulties," a University of Pennsylvania dean said, outlining a procedure used by many colleges. "In the dormitories, for about every twenty freshmen, there is a dormitory counsellor, who keeps himself aware of what is happening to the student, who knows when the student is placed on probation in any of his courses, who recognizes when the student is getting into any other source of difficulty. He may work with the student himself. If he realizes the student needs additional help, he may refer him to someone else. Each of the schools has a personnel officer who calls the student in to talk with him, or if necessary, to refer him to someone else."

By "someone else," the dean referred to the personnel of the mental health clinic. Psychiatry would seem to be used like aspirin at the colleges today. "Have a headache, son? Don't like college, eh? Then I guess you need to see a psychiatrist. . . ."

This would seem to be a symptomatic, rather than a therapeutic, treatment of the matter, undertaken with the best will in the world, but for the wrong reasons.

It may well be the purpose of a college to raise more questions than it answers. If so, we have got to understand that most questions will baffle late adolescents for no other reason than that these youngsters will lack data and experience on which to formulate a reply. If their bafflement ultimately results in an emotional response, who is being emotionally immature? The grown men who set the trap, or the innocent struggling in it? Now, when a student has been led to examine the values of society and responds with a massive rejection of society, the trap is cruel indeed. For him, the alternatives might seem to be the academic and the workaday worlds. If he can't stomach one, he is stuck with the other. If he detests both, then he is really caught, and it may take him quite a while to find, or invent for himself, some activity that gives him pleasure and provides him with a living. In any case, the student's "problem" is one *we* pose to him, and if he doesn't seem to answer it in ways that *we* find acceptable, then we say it is *his* problem.

Much of our view of the college student is colored by our preconceptions. Is the student who wishes to stay in college always more mature than the student who leaves it in sophomore year? Consider: we almost never think anything wrong with the boy who enters graduate school. But, now, let us ask college seniors why they are entering graduate school. Here are sample replies from students one meets only too often:

"To tell you the truth, I haven't any idea."

"If you can get into graduate school, you don't have to decide right away."

"I'm going to get married and go to graduate school. Money? Well, we figure she can get a job while I go. Then I'll get a job while she gets her degree. Why? Maybe we'll both teach, I don't know. There's nothing else to do, I guess."

109

"All I know is that I don't want a job."

"If I can get to graduate school, I won't get drafted. I can stay there until I'm over age."

Of all the reasons for entering upon further study, fear of the draft is the one most frequently put forth. It is correct to suspect that many students who give specific vocational reasons for going to graduate school are giving us society-pleasing rationalizations to cover this fear. The specter of the Army would seem to haunt every college boy in the land. It is not that they think they will be killed in a war, although some of them do fear they may be called to Viet Nam. Rather, they most usually say they are afraid of being brainwashed. One boy put it thus:

"The Army is brutalizing and dehumanizing."

"Was your father in the Army?" he was asked.

"Yes."

"Is he brutal? Is he a monster?"

"No, but. . . ."

"So the Army didn't brutalize him?"

"Well, he was an exception."

"Would you say that all your father's friends are brutal and monstrous? How about President Kennedy? He was in the service. Was he pretty brutal and inhuman?"

"You can't argue like that," the boy said. "For *me* the Army would be brutal and inhuman. They'd tell me what to think and what to do. You'd be stuck with some drill instructor who would hit you in the face if your shoes weren't shined, and you can't hit him back."

"Do you know of such a thing ever happening?"

"A guy in our dorm said he had a friend who was hit by a drill instructor."

"But you've never been in the Army, and you've never visited an Army post, so you have no personal knowledge of what Army life would mean to you. You assume it would be brutalizing, but the only adults you know personally—your father and his friends—seem to have survived the experience without becoming monsters. Isn't that right?"

"All I know is that it's pointless to have an Army in peacetime," the boy said. "There's never going to be another war because of the Bomb, so why *have* an Army? In the Army you have no identity, you're just a number that jumps when somebody shouts at you, and all the other guys are going to be real clods. I don't want some clod telling me what to do, pushing me around. It would just be a waste of two of the best years of my life."

Here we arrive at the heart of the matter: self-centeredness. It is perhaps ominous that so many of our most intelligent youth refuse to consider military service one of the obligations of citizenship, but see in it only an interference in their private lives. These young men are prepared to ask us to provide them with fellowships, scholarships, and grants-in-aid to enter graduate schools, not because they wish to contribute to the sum of human knowledge, but simply to dodge the draft. Who, here, seems emotionally mature? Which of them seems a Cincinnatus, willing in case of need to serve the Senate and people of Rome? Fear of the draft is also responsible for a number of college marriages. One might wonder whether fear of one kind of responsibility is the best of reasons for the assumption of another. In any case, one graduate student said:

"If they ended the draft today, the graduate schools

in this country would empty overnight—and you wouldn't be able to get hotel reservations in Reno tomorrow."

"Frankly," one professor said, "I can't say that I blame them. I really don't know how any boy can get any work done at college these days with the Army hovering over him. The students know that if they fail, they'll be sent into the Army; that when they are graduated, the Army will take them. They are afraid that if they start work on graduation, the Army will come along and take them out of their jobs. This uncertainty in their lives, this tension, must be enormously difficult to live with. I would hate to be a boy today, growing up with this fear hanging over me. Some boys will drop out of college to join the Army to get it over with, but whether they ever return to college, I do not know. We do not have many returning here. If you intend to write something about the emotional problems of college students, you must put fear of the draft high on your list."

Given such a schoolmaster, what could one expect of his students? He would seem to be living in a dream world rather than in our blood-soaked century. Yet he, like so many of his colleagues, speaks of the students' "emotional immaturity." A Columbia University counsellor ascribes students' emotional problems to the diminishing influence of family, church, and faculty. A Harvard man says young people feel insecure because neither home nor college defines the rules. Another Harvard professor says it is because society's definitions of right and wrong are inconsistent. So they say it is our fault, society's fault, not theirs, that so many of our brightest youngsters work themselves into frames of mind ranging from literal suicide to more

112

figurative escapism. They say we send disturbed young-sters to college—to which we can only reply that they seemed all right until they got there.

Well aware of a condition, if possibly mistaken as to the cause, nearly all selective colleges now permit a student in trouble to take a leave of absence for a period ranging up to two years, in order that he may resolve his problems.

"I think our fundamental attitude toward this is that the students *do* have the right to make this decision themselves, and that we will go to certain lengths in trying to explain that what they feel is the difficulty is not unique with them," one admissions officer explained. "We show them that others have faced the same kind of questions. I think we also try to point out to them the real costs that they are not including in their reckoning when they interrupt an education. We encourage them to stay with it if they possibly can, or get through to the end of the year. Then, if they still want to quit, we suggest they take only a few months, or at most, a year, off."

Dropping out for a year, he added, "is a device to maintain contact with a good student who decides to leave for good reasons, and who might very well want to return, providing he could furnish awfully good positive evidence as to why he should be re-admitted."

Permitting a student to drop out is a relatively new phenomenon in American education. It seems to have been born of the colleges' experience with World War II veterans who went to college under provisions contained in a public law. Most colleges reported that veterans earned higher grade averages than any pre-vious students, thus proving that a young man could leave formal education for as much as four years without losing his aptitude for learning, or losing much of his prior academic achievement. What permission to drop out does *not* resolve are the reasons why students wanted to quit in the first place. At best, it merely gives them new reasons for returning. In a sense, granting permission to leave seems to be an Ivy League method of passing the buck. It is tantamount to saying, "If you don't love me, it is not my fault, but yours. *You* have a real problem if you don't love *me*, so don't come back until you do." But when a student returns, it is seldom to exchange kisses with a lover. He most often returns in the mood of a man visiting a brothel—he wants what the place can offer him and intends to get it, despite the inherent imperfections of the establishment.

"Most of them will never come back to the same school if they come back at all," a California admissions officer said. "When you speak of love, you are quite right. A major trouble here is that bright kids come to us because they are in love with the college. They don't know a thing about the place, really, but they're in love with us, anyway. They're in love with the whole idea of going to college. Then, they find out it's more of the same old school work, if on a slightly higher plane, and the love affair is over. When an affair is over, it's over. Normally, it never ends with the two people remaining just good friends, but with them parting, saying, 'you bastard.' "

Perhaps most love affairs end when one or another of the lovers suddenly perceives there is a distance between the ideal and the real. The brilliant, contemplative student is often a poor collegiate risk. The U.S. Office of Education says that the unimaginative, mediocre student is much more likely to remain to be graduated. It may be perfectly true that many student problems can be traced to the gap between intellectual and emotional maturity, in the sense that if a bright but naive adolescent experiences an emotion, he can more readily magnify it into a major problem than he can if he is dull. Or it may be that his emotional reaction stems not from immaturity, but from inexperience—that he becomes frustrated because he cannot find the words or means whereby to argue dispassionately that he is bored, or exasperated, by courses that seem meaningless to him. How is he to say, unemotionally, that he is disgusted by something that society emotionally claims to be youth's greatest good?

But now there is another matter to consider. Kinsey says that late adolescence, at least for the male, is the time of greatest sexual activity. Not desire, or drive, but *activity*. Private psychiatrists, patching together the psyches of dropouts and transfer students, report that no matter what reasons the students advance for their leaving college, their fundamental problems are, in almost every instance, sexual. When a student tells a psychiatrist that his school seemed a lonely place where friendship was impossible, or that he left because his studies seemed irrelevant, or that "I left because I lacked motivation," the psychiatrist may very well suspect, "Maybe his girl said 'No.'" Emotional problems and sexual problems may be inextricably one in reality, but for the purposes of this book, it seems well to consider, separately, the sexual life of the college student.

6

Desire under the elms

Nearly all students and most faculty members today believe that sexual intercourse is not subject to moral judgment. They subscribe to psychiatry's general view that mutually-agreed-upon coitus is harmful only when the act leaves one or both partners filled with doubts, fears, and a sense of guilt.

"What I do on a date is my business and nobody else's," an eighteen-year-old Sarah Lawrence girl said.

"If two people are in love, there is nothing wrong with their going to bed together, providing nobody gets hurt," a Smith girl argued.

"There is nothing guilty about sex itself, it is just that society thinks it is guilty," a Bryn Mawr student said. "Actually, sex is just the friendliest thing you can do."

"Having sex with a boy is the only way you can really find out everything about him," a University of

116

Michigan coed explained. "Would you want to marry someone you didn't know everything about?"

"The only thing I'd miss by dropping out of college is regular sexual intercourse," a Harvard boy said. "Actually, that is the only thing keeping me here."

"Nobody expects to marry a virgin any more," a Cornell boy said. "We've progressed a lot since the days when everybody was frustrated."

These remarks may suggest to older readers that the collegiate view of sexual matters has undergone a certain modification since their own youthful days. No statistics are available to prove that the number of students who engage in intercourse has proportionately increased over the years, although there is every reason to suppose it has. But we are concerned here with collegiate beliefs, and not with an attempt to keep score. The predominant student and faculty opinion is that each student has the right to decide whether to engage in sexual intercourse, and that if a boy and girl are in love, they ought to go to bed together. On the other hand, the overwhelming opinion of college deans and psychiatrists is that most undergraduates are emotionally unready for coitus, and that they should therefore not engage in it. Official action on this belief ranges from the strictest sort of chaperonage enforced at some schools to the University of Chicago's practice of dispensing birth control pills to any coed who asks for them.* While making no moral judgment, Chicago does make every attempt to be sure that the girl really knows what she is about to do, and why, and whether she is happy with her decision. The university urges—but does not demand—that she

* As reported in *Newsweek* magazine, April 6, 1964.

talk matters over with resident psychiatrists at the school's mental health clinic.

If, without further ado, we accept the proposition that some students copulate fairly regularly; that a great many more wish they did; and that practically all of them talk incessantly about sex, we can go on to ask some questions. For example, when a girl and boy go to a motel, are they really alone? Is no one else involved? Granted, the two youngsters may be in love—whatever that means—but who are they to judge whether their sleeping together is not doing harm to one or the other of them, or to the college community? Does sexual intercourse assist or hinder the cause of scholarship? What effect does loss of virginity have on boy and girl? Does premarital intercourse lead to better selection of a mate and so to relative bliss, or does it simply lead to early boredom? Is not sexual experimentation during late adolescence a normal development, and if it is, is it any business of a college to guide or encourage it? Doubtless the answer to all these questions might seem to be, "It all depends upon the individuals involved." Very well: let us look at an individual case. Here is one that few pulp magazines, or radio soap operas, could match for the stereotyped, hearts-and-flowers witlessness displayed by all hands:

Mary Doe dropped out of an Eastern women's college during her sophomore year when she became pregnant. Learning that she was pregnant at first filled her with a great joy, for she loved John very much indeed, and he had given her every assurance that he loved her. She believed herself engaged to be married when she went to bed with him in his college room. So, she imagined they would be married now that she

118

was pregnant. She reasoned that his family had plenty of money, as hers had; so no doubt their families would be glad to support them. She did not mind the idea of dropping out of college to find an apartment in his college town, because she had gone to college to find a husband, anyway. Of course, John would stay on in school until he received his degree, because a man must have a degree if he would hope to support a wife.

So Mary went gaily back to Cleveland to tell her family the good news. Their reaction was to telephone John's family in New York, with a view to setting an immediate wedding date. Their call caused some embarrassment, for it was the first time John's parents had heard of Mary Doe.

"Who are these people? Who is this girl—some gold digger?" John's father asked him. "Would you mind telling me what this is all about?"

Mary was a friend of his, John explained. No, he had never at any time promised to marry anyone, because "I told her I had to go through college first. Sure, we *thought* maybe someday we might get married if things worked out O.K. and if we were still in love when we got out of school, but it wasn't any more than that. I mean, she said she loved me, so I, ah, you know. . . ."

No, John told his father, he hadn't taken precautions because "I mean, Pop, if a girl says O.K., she'll come to your room, doesn't that mean she's wearing her diaphragm?"

John's father relayed his son's gallant reply to Mary's family, and the bottom dropped out of Mary's world. John's father had refused to consent to a marriage. He said he would contest a paternity suit. Mary's first frantic thought was that she would have the baby, anyway. Perhaps after the baby was born, the unwilling grandfather would relent. She could not accept the idea that John did not want to marry her.

"You're going to have an abortion at eleven o'clock Tuesday morning at the hospital," Mary's father told her.

"No! I won't!" Mary said. "I would rather have the baby and put it up for adoption!"

So Mary had an abortion at eleven o'clock Tuesday morning. It was performed by the obstetrician who had delivered her nineteen years ago. She returned to college the following year to resume her education.

The point of all this is not that going to a college boy's room can lead a college girl to the operating table. Rather, it is that what happened to Mary was a source of acute concern to more than two adolescents. Of course Mary was the principal victim, and the full effects of her tragedy probably remain to be seen. For no woman ever surrenders her virginity in a wholly casual way, and, more important, no woman can ever have an abortion, suffer a miscarriage, or see her baby die without having that experience do some lasting damage to her mental equilibrium. Mary's pregnancy was a source of anguish to both her parents and to John's, and it may even have given John something to think about. But, more to the point, it affected a number of innocent bystanders—Mary's classmates, who had been kept fully informed of every stage of Mary's romance.

Early on, she had told them she was not a virgin and had described in detail her sexual relationship with John. This inspired one girl with a thrill of horror, and may be a reason why that girl seems to dress in as repellent a manner as could be conceived; why she has no dates. At least two other girls were led to intimate they were not virgins, although they were, and to become technical virgins upon the next week end. A technical virgin, in today's campus jargon, means a girl who may lie naked in bed with a boy and engage with him to orgasm in all forms of sexual activity except the procreative. ("I have this problem with my girl," said one Princeton victim of technical virginity. "I have this sexual appetite, but all she ever gives me are appetizers.")

When Mary told her friends she was pregnant and would doubtless now be married, her friends wanted to Do Something. They happily thought in terms of bridal showers and baby showers ("It will be the class baby, won't it?") until a long, hysterical letter from Mary inspired them to want to Do Something Else. Three wanted to take turns calling John and telling him a thing or two. One wanted to hire a lawyer to sue John's parents. A movement was undertaken, then abandoned, to solicit a subscription for Mary's abortion. All this flutter in the dovecote was not without its effects on the girls' schoolwork. Emotionally involved in their friend's problem, they added its burden to those they already carried. Endless conversations were built about Mary, virginity, abortions, trial marriage, and How Far Do You Go With A Boy. Anyone who thinks that nineteen-year-old girls are past the point of such discussions is unduly cynical. If the girls had put the same effort into their schoolwork that they put into worry over Mary, they might all have made the dean's list. As it was, two wound up on probation, and one of them considered dropping out. Persuading her to stay on required additional woman-hours of dormitory conversation.

Perhaps the most astonishing feature of this ridiculous melodrama is the fact that all participants—John, the girls, the two families—are highly intelligent people of whom greater wisdom might have been expected. But the case serves the point that intellect and sexual behavior do not always go together, and that when late adolescents fool around with sex, most of them do not know what they are doing.

Mary's tragedy might have remained exclusively private if college were a normal community. But a college is a collection of adolescents left largely on their own resources. Most of today's faculty members have little more than an impersonal classroom acquaintance with their students. This is particularly true at a large university. It is less true at a small college, but the general rule is that the college teacher is no longer—if he ever was—the kindly, wise old professor who is the inspiring friend of youth, to whom the students can apply for advice. He is much more likely to be a smug young graduate student single-mindedly pursuing a degree, or a self-centered young associate professor looking for another job. Unless they consult the college's resident psychiatrist, the students must look to one another for guidance at one of the times of life when guidance would seem most necessary—which would generally mean that the blind would lead the blind. This was certainly true of Mary and her friends who, locked away in a little world of their own, tried to solve Mary's problem with her, with the result that they all burst into tears over it.

Closely connected to campus sexuality, if not one of the conducive factors, is the unreality of the collegiate world. As the preceding chapters suggested, it is a world of vivid tensions, and sexual relationship might seem to ease these tensions and solace the lonely.

"To go to bed with a girl because you want a sense of status and she wants a sense of security does not strike me as being a particularly mature, mutual act of love," one private psychiatrist said. "But this is what is happening in most cases. The usual boy-girl relationship involves an immature boy seeking a mother-image. Mama isn't around any more, so the girl becomes a substitute Mama. She's going to pat him and hug him and soothe him when he's all worried about those dreadful old studies, and then best of all, she's going to give him something Mama never did. I don't know what percentage of campus marriages last, but I do know that a good many of them end in divorce shortly after graduation, and I believe some of them end when the boy finally grows up and doesn't want a Mama any more, and when the girl gets over playing with dolls and starts looking for a man."

Incidentally, to understand just what divorce can mean to some of the nation's best young minds, consider the couple who met early in freshman year, married, had a child in the spring, and then were divorced. The boy spent the summer on a youth hostel trip through Europe; the girl gave the baby to an adoption agency and took a summer job as a hospital volunteer because "I feel we should help other people." This past year they were both back in college as sophomores, where they often met at the same parties because their circle of friends had not changed, and their relationship was that of two youngsters who had once dated steadily, but who did so no longer, and their friends think none the less of them.

"The marriage didn't work out," one of their friends said.

And the baby?

"Who's to say that the people who adopt children aren't better parents than if they were the real parents?" one student asked. "The most religious guy is the convert."

It would seem that a quick mind is never at a loss for a rationalization.

It would also seem that our youth are pursuing what they believe to be their newly invented sexual freedom somewhat lugubriously, for as a San Francisco professor said, "The sad thing is that so many of these kids act like old married couples.

"You really wonder if they find sex fun," he said. "Let me tell you about one couple living together on a houseboat about twenty minutes away from here by car. They commute to the campus. She is a big blond motherly girl of Scandinavian descent. The boy is a little dark New York Jew with the cynical attitude of a cabin boy. They have a college post office box number so their parents won't know where they are living. But there's nothing joyous or Bohemian about their household. There are no beaded curtains, or wine bottles with candles in them on check tablecloths. There's nothing nautical. Instead, what could have been an exotic houseboat, they've made into the most unexciting, drab, dismal little working-class flat you've ever seen. They have a kind of pride of poverty—how-you-can-eat-four-course-meals-for-43¢-a-day kind of thing. They buy furniture from the Goodwill Industries, and their clothes at J. C. Penney's. She is ultra domestic, keeping everything spotless. Seeing him varnishing a chair is like watching a guy working in his

basement hobby room after a tough day at the office.
They entertain constantly, but there are no wild parties. Instead, it's the couple in for dinner, with beer
and shoptalk afterwards.

"They are just two kids with nothing really in common who are playing house," the professor concluded.
"Underneath it all you can see what it is. She really
wants to be a domestic homebody and has found
security and an outlet in having a boy-husband she
doesn't care about, and he has found a mother and a
status symbol. The boy with the most status is the one
who is shacked up."

Playing house would seem an apt term for many
less permanent campus relationships, and it seems to
be the girl who does most of the playing. In most
cases, if she is not the actual aggressor (which she
often is) she is at least the more active partner. If the
boy lives off campus, the pattern is that she comes to
his apartment to tidy it up, cook the supper, do the
dishes. She is the one who provides the contraceptive.
(One may say, *Well she might*, for it is she who would
become pregnant. The point, however, is that the boy
today—unlike the college boy of the 1930's—does not
so often take some responsibility for making sure that
a contraceptive is used.) At the end of the evening,
she often as not walks back to the women's dormitory
alone. Inasmuch as it is a fact of nature that boys
bring far less of an emotional commitment to bed
with them than girls do, one sometimes wonders just
what the college girl really gets out of this activity.
How much psychic and physical risk does she run,
for how little real reward?

With narrow respect for scholarship—the ostensible
reason why people attend college—students often

125

argue that a sexual relationship is conducive to good grades. To be sure, fear of pregnancy can wreck a girl's schoolwork. But students say that contraception minimizes this fear and that a greater one is that of not having dates. In today's collegiate world, where sexual intercourse is widely believed to be nothing more than a natural act, necessary to good mental health, and always permissible providing the couple imagine themselves to be in love and if they use contraceptives and conduct the affair in private, it is popularly believed that a girl is having intercourse if she dates one boy exclusively. If she does, then she is supposed to realize that she is attractive to men and will not die a spinster. With fear of spinsterhood removed from her mind, she is now supposed to be the more free to devote her full attention to her schoolwork. That such a conclusion may be psychological nonsense is neither here nor there. The point is, such is a belief that many students share.

The undergraduate world likewise presumes that a boy's grades will improve if he enjoys regular sexual intercourse, for his conquest is supposed to furnish proof of his virility, otherwise set his mind at rest, and at least assure him that somebody likes him, even if nobody else at the college does.

No one has attempted to make a study to show whether non-virgins earn higher grades than other students. Some teachers believe that students who date steadily tend to earn higher grades than those who do not, and that they are less likely to drop out of college. If true, this does not establish a relationship between dating and grades. It might simply mean that bright students find more time to date than dull students do.

126

Despite popular undergraduate belief, we cannot always presume that steady dating implies intercourse. There is no question that there is a pressure on a college girl to regard virginity as a badge of immaturity and to become the sexual partner of her steady date, but there is a question as to how many college girls actually yield to this pressure.

It would seem safe to say that they talk a great deal about sex, but whether all the conversationalists speak from experience is quite another matter.

"We heard that ninety-five per cent of Sarah Lawrence girls will come across on the first date," one Harvard boy said.

"But we got stuck with the five per cent who don't," his friend complained.

"There's a lot more virginity around than you would expect," a Reed professor said.

His view is particularly interesting, inasmuch as Reed College is so small as to resemble a family group in which students and professors seem to live as equals, and since undergraduates who do not go to Reed enviously imagine Reed to be a center of free love.

"Three girls who live together here each came to me separately," the Reed professor said. "Each one said that her roommates weren't virgin, and that they had told her she should go to bed with a man, too, but each of them told me that she didn't want to do this yet, and did this mean there was something wrong with her?"

If much of collegiate sex is just talk about sex, there is no doubt that the conversations are becoming increasingly frank and increasingly conducted in mixed company. Incessant talk can create pressure. It encourages experiment. It can create anxiety and self-reproach in the mind of a gullible student who imagines that everyone else is leading a vivid sexual life while his or her only outlet at the moment is masturbation.

The entire problem is complicated by the fact that while the late adolescent male actually completes more sexual acts per week than he ever will again, the late adolescent girl has still some years to wait before she is psychologically and physiologically as eager for intercourse as he is now. But bearing in upon her from a hundred sources are commands that she go to bed, anyway. She has only to look at the outside world to see a sex-obsessed society. Most motion pictures, all manner of advertising, practically every novel, the vast majority of newspaper feature articles, and nearly all drama back to Punch and Judy concern men and women going to bed together or wanting to do so. She has been encouraged to put on a lugubrious preteen bra when her breasts were buds; has been car-pooled to dancing class in nylon stockings and lipstick before mastering long division; has been thrust into quasi-adult social relationships all the way from junior high school to college; has inescapably absorbed in high school the idea that her chances of a happy life are going to be in direct proportion to her ability as a sexual athlete, and now, arrived in college, surrounded by ardent males and given every encouragement and opportunity, she is practically ordered to produce or admit personal failure as a woman. Something deep inside her may clamor "But it is too soon! I'm not ready yet!" and if so, then we may conclude that she has a problem.

For their part, boys have a problem, too. Raised in the same erotic culture, more sensitive to its stimulation than girls, and in full command of their sexual powers, boys are impelled to prove themselves. Proving one's sexual ability provides at least one kind of self-assurance. Granted, work may be a means of sublimating a sex drive, but the collegiate world offers only academic work, which is hardly everybody's cup of tea. In all seriousness, consider the plight of a bright boy who badly wants to get on with the business of living his life, but who finds himself marooned in the artificial collegiate world instead. Where and how is he to prove himself the man he feels himself to be? Does he not have a problem? But if he found a more complaisant girl, would she really provide him with the answer?

As this is being written, there is an uproar in the daily press and monthly journals over campus morality. It centers largely around the practice in many selec tive colleges of allowing boys and girls to entertain one another in their dormitory rooms. It seems that the press has discovered that when a boy takes a girl into his room, he hangs a towel or necktie on the doorknob to serve as a Do Not Disturb sign. Judging the collegiate world by the standards of the outside world, we might all presume that whenever a man and woman enter a bedroom together and close the door, they go to bed. This is by no means always the case with college students, but the question has been asked whether it is wise to grant boys and girls the opportunity of sharing a bedroom for a date.

"From the day that Harvard first let girls into student rooms, they had all this trouble coming to them," one weekly magazine quoted a woman dean of students as saying.

But what is "all this trouble?" Admittedly, pregnancy out of wedlock is trouble. *Newsweek* magazine reported that, at one Eastern women's college, a dozen girls in one year engaged in shotgun weddings and another six had abortions. The incidence of premarital pregnancy on campus is increasing. A question might be asked as to whether the eighteen girls at that women's college would have become pregnant had the college issued contraceptive pills, and if so, whether these particular girls would have taken them. Once upon a time, the college boy used to visit the town girl for sexual purposes, rather than the college girl he intended to marry. Today, the town girl is going to college, too. We can assume a certain number of premarital pregnancies in any random sample of young women. But since this number will be trifling, compared with the total number of female college students, what else is "all this trouble" about?

It would seem that the major problem stems from the fact that the collegiate world is a corral full of erotic adolescents. College deans may maintain from here until next Thursday morning that most undergraduates are too immature to fool around with sex, but the most casual glance at the history of human behavior, from Creation to date, indicates that late adolescents are going to fool around with it anyway. They have sexual problems. A question put to the colleges is whether it is any business of the college to help students cope with those problems. To try to keep them apart, by limiting their opportunities to engage in intercourse, or by expelling them if they do, is one way of not answering the question. But is it any better answer to provide adolescents with bedrooms wherein they may work out their sexual problems by themselves? The students, with some faculty support, say that it is. They argue that the decent privacy of one's own dormitory room is infinitely preferable to the cynical impersonality of the public motel to which they must otherwise resort. In any event, they say, no one is going to be able to legislate sexuality out of human behavior.

Perhaps the most lucid thought on a murky scene was that of a high school teacher who said, "A child's best chaperone is his own character." If any college girl's father believes that students are not ready to be the judges of themselves, but should follow his mature wisdom instead, he would be well advised to compile a list of all the married adults of his acquaintance. Then he might ask himself what he knows of their sexual lives, and of his own. Sober contemplation might convince him that today's knowing children are comparative innocents in the art of making trouble for themselves. Indeed, the sexual life of the undergraduate will probably be seen as far more honest than that of the alumnus.

It is not the province of this book to suggest what the official collegiate attitude should be with regard to the sexual life of the undergraduate. Rather, the intention here is to demonstrate that undergraduates do lead sexual lives and to report on the current trend of undergraduate opinion on the matter. No one knows whether engaging in sexual intercourse tends to reduce or magnify the tensions of college life; whether it tends to raise or lower grade averages. No one knows whether *not* engaging in intercourse is helpful or harmful to the undergraduate. Examples of each point may be found: we are left with a sheaf of reports which show nothing more than that human beings are infinitely variable; that each must be considered separately; that a norm is an abstract term to which no particular individual conforms. But we can certainly say that having sexual relations, or not having them, powerfully affects each undergraduate's general outlook. His view of himself in the collegiate world, and his efficiency therein, is largely determined by whatever peace, truce, or armistice he has made with his sexual self.

Close inquiry into the reasons why a student transfers or drops out of college will invariably be answered in emotional terms, or at least in terms highly colored by emotion, and Freudian psychiatrists say that these emotions will be rooted in the student's sexuality. For example, no dropout is more common than the boy whose difficulties can be traced to a disappointing love affair, or the girl who leaves college because she has now snared the husband she went to college to entrap. Nor is any transfer student more common than he, or she, whose sexual life has seemed meager, and who wishes to try again somewhere else. But before we conclude that all able students who voluntarily leave a college do so because of sexual uproar, we had best remember that their sexual dissatisfactions most usually gnaw at them from beneath the threshold of consciousness, while their conscious minds seize upon the many more apparent shortcomings of college life, intellectualizing these into reasons for leaving.

7

Greener pastures

Most college professors say they cannot remember a
time when so many students transferred from one
college to another so blithely as they do today. An
exception was a medievalist whose memory was a little
longer than those of his confreres.

"We now have something recalling the days of the
wandering scholars, drifting from one university town
to another in pursuit of learning," he said. "I see nothing wrong with this. I think the experience is valuable.
Why shouldn't they carry their search from place to
place?"

"What we're seeing is a sort of shaking-down," another professor suggested. "They come to us and find
that we expect them to do hard work, and they want
to find another school where they will not have to
work so hard."

He implied no criticism. He thought the process a

healthy one. If weaker students transferred out of his school, however, such is not the usual case among other first-rate colleges and universities.

"Sophomore year is the one when there are more transfers than any other," a dean of students said. "During the first three months of the academic year, students will literally be lined up outside my door, waiting to see me about transfer. No, they will not be just those in academic difficulties. Here, unfortunately, it is the top of the class who want to leave us."

"For some students, transfer seems to be a thing to do," another professor said. "We have—in fact, many colleges now have—scholarship funds for transfers. Mind you, the better colleges will not accept transfer students who have poor grades. Because of attrition during the first two years, there will always be room for transfers into the upper classes of most colleges, and why shouldn't that room be used? The good students know the room is there at the good schools, and many students will use this university as a means of gaining entrance to a selective college which might have refused them admission as freshmen."

"I often wonder if the big national scholarships have not invited transfer," an admissions officer said. "Transfer is a thing like divorce; if you've done it once, you'll do it again, and it is not unusual to find students who have gone to four colleges in four years, often able to do so because of their National Merit or Westinghouse Science scholarships, which move with them."

Implicit in the faculty view is an appraisal of the transfer *as a student*, but it may be more accurate to suggest that the reasons why boys and girls change schools may have nothing whatsoever to do with scholarship.

134

"This place is Hungry Hill," one girl said of her small women's college. "We're miles and miles from anywhere, and I mean it's not that I'm boy crazy or anything like that, but it's just that, you know, it would be more *normal* at a coed school."

Her explanation of why she wanted to transfer was close to the mark, but not altogether candid. It seems that she thoroughly enjoyed her first year at Hungry Hill, but during the Christmas vacation of her sophomore year, her heart was captured by a boy from Northwestern. So she has now applied for transfer to Northwestern, telling her parents nothing about the boy, but rather that she feels a women's college "is too isolated from reality" and that she wants the challenge of attending a large university in a different section of the country.

New love affairs, broken love affairs, disappointments both real and imaginary, personal inadequacies, and simple youthful wanderlust might well inspire as many transfers as newly discovered scholarly goals. One reason for a number of transfers might be that improved means of transportation, from jet flights to new highways, have made the nation smaller and transfer easier. In an affluent age of commonplace marvels, no one's home is more than a day away from any college, so that distance and expense are no longer factors determining one's choice of schools. Another reason for transfer might be plain boredom and the illusion of the greener grass. Perhaps a reason why the faculty generally presumes that students wish to transfer for scholarly reasons is that the students tell them so. What else are the students to say? Just as on his application form for admission, so on the application form for transfer, the wise child will parrot the answers that school and society expect. At this point, let us look at one boy's case in some detail:

Bob is a well-built blond, blue-eyed, wholesome-looking son of wealthy parents who have a strong religious orientation. He, too, has a more serious respect for ethical matters than most of us have. His aptitude and achievement test scores (ranging from the high 600's to the low 700's) place him in the upper 2 per cent of all college applicants. He was graduated with honors from a first-rate Eastern private boarding school. He could have gone to any college he wished, for in addition to his family's money, his scholarly abilities, and the reputation of his preparatory school, he also proved himself a leader in student affairs and in athletics. So, Bob would appear to be the All-American Boy—not a goody-goody, but a straightforward, decent lad of singular promise and background. He is well spoken and he seems to be a mature, thoughtful boy as compared with others his age. He is nineteen, has just completed his freshman year at college, and now wishes to transfer from a Midwestern college to an Eastern university—his choice is wavering between Princeton and Harvard. Here follows the transcript of a tape-recorded interview:

Q. Why did you go to Oberlin in the first place?

A. I felt I wanted a coed school with a high academic standing.

Q. What was wrong with Swarthmore?

A. Well, my home is in Philadelphia, and I wanted to get away from home, and my headmaster recommended Oberlin highly—his daughter went there. I visited the campus. Unfortunately, none of the kids were there at the time. But I'd known people who had gone there, and it was a good campus.

Q. If you wanted a coed school with a high academic standing, why didn't you go to Harvard?

A. I went to school in New England. I wanted to get away from the Ivy schools. I didn't want to go to Princeton—my father went there, and my cousins went there. I just didn't want to go there.

Q. But you have now applied for transfer to Princeton?

A. Yes. I tried to get in there, but they wouldn't give me an application form.

Q. Then you don't want a coed school any more?

A. Yes, I like it. I still like it. But Oberlin's hardly a coed school, in that sense. I mean, nobody takes time off to have any fun, and the college itself isn't set up much to have fun.

Q. Do you think you have to have fun when you go to college?

A. Well, that's a phase of it, certainly.

Q. But Princeton isn't a coed school. Why did you want to go there now?

A. Well, Princeton has a very good, you know, English Department.

Q. What is a *good English Department?*

A. What is it?

Q. Yes.

A. I don't know that I could answer that, really. Certainly, it's one that has made a reputation over the years and still has the men who made the reputation.

Q. The reputation for what?

A. I don't know what you mean.

Q. I mean, what is the reputation that Princeton's English Department has made? On what, specifically, is it based?

A. All I know is that it's just a good one.

Q. Who told you that?

A. Mr. Johnson would uphold that; Mr. Knightsbridge told me that. [Bob is naming two of his preparatory school masters.] And other people have told me that both Princeton and Harvard have good English Departments.

Q. Why do you want a good English Department?

A. Well, if I'm going to major in it, I want a good department.

Q. Why are you majoring in it?

A. I've not really decided what I'm going to do with it.

Q. For instance, do you have any particular reason why you might want to study the 17th century lyrical English poets as different from the 17th century dramatic English poets?

A. No. If I majored in English, I'd probably take the more modern things.

Q. Would it surprise you if I told you that the reputation of the English Department at Princeton is predicated on their excellence in the 17th century lyrical poets?

A. It wouldn't surprise me, no.

Q. Well, is this what you think would be best offered to you by Princeton?

A. No-o-o. . . .

Q. As a matter of fact, I don't know *what* made the reputation of Princeton's English Department, or even what that reputation is. Do *you* have any real idea what it is, other than what somebody whose opinion you respect said that he thought the reputation was good?

A. No.

Q. Do you have any serious interest in scholarship?

138

A. Ah . . . I'm interested in English.

Q. This is a serious academic discipline. What phase of English do you wish to pursue? What has captured your imagination?

A. Well, more, I guess, modern authors.

Q. What kind of modern authors, who write what?

A. People like Dylan Thomas, who write poetry, plays.

Q. Would you like to write poetry and plays?

A. Not that I want to write them. I might be interested in going into teaching.

Q. And you want to teach poetry and plays in particular?

A. Not in particular, I wouldn't think, but I would want to be familiar with them. I would want to take the courses in the 17th century, too. I guess you have to, in order to know what you're doing.

Q. And Princeton could make you more familiar with these things than any other college?

A. All I can tell you is what I've heard.

Q. Other people have told you that it's good? People whose opinions you respect?

A. Yes.

Q. What I'm getting at here is that you have no personal measurement; no way to have a personal measurement as to what constitutes a good English Department.

A. I wouldn't know, myself. Certainly, I have to rely on what other people say, if I respect their opinions.

Q. Now here you respected the opinion of your headmaster and went to Oberlin. Would you take his advice again?

A. Well, that would depend on what we were talking about, I guess. I mean, he had no personal reasons for telling me to go to Oberlin—all he said was that it was a good school and that his daughter had gone there, and I had no objection to the quality of the education I'd get there.

Q. If you have no objection to the quality of the education, why do you want to transfer?

A. I don't like the whole atmosphere. I think the kids pressure themselves more than they have to. The college itself isn't set up for anything but education. Which is a mistake, I think.

Q. You mean the college emphasizes academic training, as in scholarship?

A. Yes.

Q. And you're not a scholar?

A. Well, no, I'm not saying that. But I wouldn't say that I am. But I would say that there are other things that go along with an education, that are just as important.

Q. Then you found there was an overbalance at Oberlin? That the other kids were so wrapped up in their scholarship that they didn't have time for other things that would interest you?

A. More or less. Not that they had an overpowering interest in scholarship, it was just that that was all they were interested in.

Q. Give me an example.

A. All right. When we got there freshman week, the dean said he'd like to see everybody have a date on Saturday night. That was their policy, and they encouraged it, or words to that effect. Well, on any Saturday night, all the lights in the dormitories are lit, and the kids are in there, studying. And even if you had a date on Saturday night, there just isn't all that much to do. Oberlin is just a little crossroads, and there's really very little to do in the town, so most kids just study.

Q. Would it surprise you to know that the same thing could be said with respect to Harvard—not that there's nothing to do in the Boston area or on the Harvard campus itself—but with respect to the fact that most of the kids study like hell? And that they spend much more of their time on that than on anything else?

A. Well, I'm sure they do. They do at Oberlin, too, but I mean the crowd at Harvard would be drawn from a different *background*.

Q. What kind of background do the kids at Oberlin have?

A. A lot of them come from public high schools, where in order to get into Oberlin, they had to work all the time, and they just continue it in college, even though it isn't necessary there. And I've heard—I don't know whether this is true or not—that Admissions has been trying to draw the kind of people who normally would have applied to the Eastern schools, and I think that these are primarily the ones who are dissatisfied, and who are leaving.

Q. Because it's a pokey little place out in the middle of nowhere?

A. Because they're not satisfied with what they find there.

Q. What do they find?

A. Just work. That's about all. And a lot of Midwestern kids.

Q. What's wrong with the Midwestern kids?

A. Nothing, really. But they're just not all that great.

Q. Do you find the work at Oberlin significantly deeper than the work you did in prep school?

A. No. I don't think it's any harder, no.

Q. How are your grades?

A. I have a B average.

Q. Do you have a steady girl?

A. No.

Q. Would you like to have one?

A. Well, it might be pretty nice. But some guys have steady girls, and I guess they're pretty much frustrated.

Q. Do you have any close friends at Oberlin?

A. Yep. But all of my close friends are leaving, quickly.

Q. All of them?

A. I wouldn't say all of them.

Q. What are some of their reasons for leaving?

A. Just about the same reasons I have. They just can't stand the general atmosphere of the college and the waste of their social life—I mean, there just *isn't any* social life.

Q. What about the course of studies you have taken? Do they satisfy you?

A. No, I'm dissatisfied with them. I'm taking courses I have to take to fulfill the general requirement, and, well, the courses I have to take, well, they're just not satisfying.

Q. But you're getting good grades in them?

A. Yes.

Q. What do you think of the teaching there? How does it measure up to your prep school teaching?

A. There isn't any teaching, really. The courses are mostly lectures, with very few classroom discussion periods. You go to lectures with two or three hundred kids in a lecture hall and you read books and write papers, with almost no classroom instruction. It just made me mad, because I'd rather do some things on my own, instead of just vomiting back to them what they said in the lectures.

Q. Do you know what it is you want to do, either in college or in later life?

A. Nope.

Q. But you think that among the things you might like to do, perhaps, is to teach?

A. Yep.

Q. And what is your view of what a college education should be?

A. Well, first of all, I guess, you have to stress the academic part of it, that's the most important thing, after all, that's what you go there to get, but you certainly have to have a social life that goes along with it. I mean, you can't be completely academic.

Q. But what is the purpose of a college education—let me put it that way?

A. For one thing, I guess it is to help you know more about what you are, and what other people are.

Q. And college is the only place you can find this out? You can't find this out anywhere else, as well?

A. I guess you could say education is absolute. I don't really know. I wouldn't say you had to go to college to get educated, though. And I certainly wouldn't say that all the people who come out of college are educated. I suppose getting an education is a primary reason for going to college. I suppose there are a lot of secondary reasons, although I haven't really thought about them.

Q. What are some secondary reasons, now that you are thinking about them?

A. I suppose a lot of women go to college to get married.

Q. Would you take the view that you should go to college in order to be able to make money at a future time?

A. I would say this is not what I'm thinking of at the present, although I would certainly say it would help, anyway. I've been talking with a lot of kids, asking them why they got here, and they say so they can get a better job. I think that might be something you can consider about, but I don't think it should be a primary aim.

Q. Your fundamental complaint against Oberlin, however, is lack of social life?

A. Well, plus the English, yeah.

Q. What is specifically wrong with the English courses that you are taking at Oberlin?

A. I'm not taking any, yet. But I've heard from a lot of kids who have gone through it, and even my headmaster said that his daughter had told him, that the English status here doesn't look very good.

Q. Some kids will say the same thing about Harvard or Princeton.

A. Well, I imagine that you could say that anywhere. I guess the general education that I'd get at Oberlin wouldn't be any better or worse than I'd get at Harvard.

Q. Therefore, you want to leave Oberlin because you feel that its English Department is not so good, on the basis of hearsay evidence, and you want to transfer somewhere else, where again on the basis of hearsay, the English Department appears to be better?

A. Well, I suppose you could get a good education at any English Department, although it is something

144

to consider, but I just can't take the atmosphere out there. The education's fine, if that's what you want, but I think there should be something more to college than just the academic.

Q. Let me sum this up. You say you are not a scholar, and that you want an education, and that you can get an education at college, although you do not have to go college to become educated. You don't know yet what you want to do, either in college or in later life. You accepted the opinion of a man whose judgment you respect, and went to Oberlin. You found that the work was no more difficult than the work you had been doing in high school and that there was no more of it. You are disappointed with the social life and with the English Department, although since you have taken no English courses there, you know nothing about those courses except what other kids have told you. Now, you have found that, with respect to yourself, the advice your headmaster gave you did not apply. So you want to transfer to another school, about whose English Department you know nothing, other than that Mr. Johnson and Mr. Knightsbridge, whose opinions you respect, say that it is good. You don't know, do you, whether what Mr. Johnson and Mr. Knightsbridge like will please you. Do you? The only thing you really know is that while you respect your headmaster's opinions, it turned out that his advice was wrong in your case. Isn't that correct?

A. Yes, I guess you could say that.

Q. Is your father paying for your college education?

A. I pay $600 of it. The bill is $2,600.

Q. In other words, you are asking your father to pay out $8,000 over four years, to send you to college. Why are you going to college?

145

A. I don't know why I'm going to college, to tell you the truth.

Q. So you are asking your father to spend $8,000 on something—that is, you don't know why you're doing it, and so far, you haven't liked it, but you think it is perfectly all right for your father to pay out $8,000 on what amounts to buying a pig in a poke? Let me try again: You don't know why you are going to college. You don't know what you really want to study. The only thing you know about college is that you went to one that you knew only from hearsay, and that you didn't like it. Now, you are asking somebody to send you to another one that you know nothing about except from hearsay. You want to transfer from one English Department you know nothing about to another English Department you know nothing about, simply because somebody said one is bad and somebody else said the other is good. Is that right?

Before Bob could answer, a Harvard student entered the room, and the next question was put to him:

Q. Here we have a guy who says the social life at his college is nonexistent because the kids are studying instead of dating on Saturday night, and, besides, there isn't much of anywhere to go. He says he wants to major in English but he doesn't know why, and that he doesn't like his English Department, but then it turns out he has never taken any of its courses. He wants to go to another college where he's heard the English Department is better, although he hasn't taken any of its courses, either. But what all this really boils down to, is that he wants his father to help him get a date. So he's thinking of Harvard because it has a good reputation, and because it's coed and there's more to do in the Boston area than at Oberlin. Now: If a guy tells you he really doesn't think he's a scholar, and that he doesn't really know why he's going to college anyway, and that he doesn't know what he wants to do in life or in school, and if he objects to kids hitting the books instead of dating on Saturday, do you think he ought to go to Harvard?

A. Hell, no.

Q. Why not?

A. Because if you think the guys at Oberlin study, wait till you've seen the guys at Harvard. There isn't any real place there for a guy who doesn't know what he wants to do, or why he's there.

Q. Well, this guy knows one thing: he knows what he doesn't like. He knows that he's dissatisfied where he is, even if he isn't altogether sure why.

A. Then he ought to get out of it. Look, Bob, why don't you wait until the end of your sophomore year before making up your mind? Don't you see more of the upperclassmen dating than the freshmen?

A. Come to think of it, I guess they do, yes.

Q. Well, why don't you wait another term to see how it goes? Then, if it's still no good, ask for a leave of absence. Leave in good standing. Now, during your leave, figure out some good reasons for wanting to go to a specific school, or some good reasons for leaving or staying at Oberlin. Get a job at something you really like to do, or think you'd like to do, and then figure out whether you shouldn't go back to college, or whether you don't really need to go at all.

The ensuing discussion among the interviewer and the two boys arrived at the conclusion that college is generally a good thing, although not an end-all, be-all; that there was nothing magical about a four-year term. They agreed there was no reason, really, why one should attend college for four consecutive years in order to get out of any particular college what it has to offer him. It was felt that while a college degree is helpful, and good for most people to possess, the woods were full of people who lack degrees, but who are nevertheless leading happy, effective lives. It was also agreed that one might as well have a college degree as not, so that if one's objections are really minor, one should put up with them. At one point, Bob said that going to college was a good thing "because it puts off a decision. You can always go to graduate school and put off a decision for a couple more years." He said this as if in jest, but in rueful sincerity.

The important thing about Bob is that he is *not* a medieval scholar, wandering from university to university in search of learning. Instead, I suggest that he is typical of the majority of youngsters whose tested aptitudes and scholarly achievements place them within the charmed circle of the nation's youthful intellectual elite.

Bob is a good-natured, poised, intelligent boy who has nothing to think about; i.e., he lacks experience and information on which to use his brains. He is at least as emotionally and socially mature as the majority of nineteen-year-olds of his social and intellectual class. He is going through adolescence on as even a keel as anyone has a right to expect. He will obviously be effective in adult life, no matter whether he completes his college education or not, if he merely continues to be what, to a great extent, he already is: a constructive citizen, considerate and just.

Like practically all of his age and present state of education, Bob has no real idea who he is or why he is doing what he does. He is very much interested in

148

finding out, and a cloud of honest question marks seems to lie around his head.

The things that boys like Bob need to know will not be found in the curriculum of any college on earth. Home, school, and society have given Bob a great many ready-to-wear answers that encase him in an armor that has as many layers as an onion. This armor not only prevents the outside world from getting in at him, but it also prevents his seeing the outside world as a whole. Further, it limits his movements. So he is involved in trying to strip the layers away, one by one, testing each to determine whether he really wants or needs it. He is now examining for himself the notion that a college education is an indispensable good. He is questioning the validity of his assumption that he should major in English; become a teacher. The fact that he wants to transfer indicates his honest doubt, but the belief that transferring out of one first-rate college into another first-rate college is a panacea for all disappointments is merely another of convention's onion rings. Bob must divest himself of all the onion rings and look into a mirror in order to know who is making the trip. The mirror will show him a handsome, bright, and decent boy who rather badly wants a girl.

To return to the phenomenon of transfer, perhaps the most interesting aspect is that almost no one sees much wrong in the idea of students moving from one campus to another. Instead of sitting down with a boy to find out what his real reasons for leaving are, much less taking a boy aside and talking to him like a Dutch uncle, a college dean will most often wish him Godspeed. No one seems to say, You made your bed—now lie in it. No one seems to speak to the virtue of finishing a job, once begun. No on seems to care. When parents express their doubt that Tom should leave M.I.T. for Purdue, they are most often given reasons why Tom *should*. If it should be discovered that Tom wants to leave because he is unhappy, then the dean will speak to the point of Tom's happiness. No one doubts that a happy student is likely to be more productive than a dejected one, but no one seems willing to study the anatomy of happiness, or to question the relative values of different productions.

Certainly, this is not an age wherein many people believe that a greater future happiness can be gained at the necessary expense of present drudgery. This is an age of fly now, pay later. Perhaps the hydrogen bomb helps make it so—an age of present happiness without a future. In any event, the trend on campus is clear enough:

"There's a regular traffic pattern between here and Berkeley," a Reed senior said. "A lot of Eastern kids come out here and say, 'My God, there's San Francisco down the coast,' and Berkeley and San Francisco and the Bay area seem kind of exotic and so much more attractive than staying here, writing papers."

And so, too, there is a regular two-way traffic pattern between the small colleges and the large universities; between the rigorous colleges and the easy ones; also between institutions of equal caliber. In nearly every case of which the author has personal knowledge, the pursuit of happiness, not knowledge, is the reason for transfer, but it is not apt to be discovered by the college authorities. When it is, however, then it is less likely to be questioned than an expressed desire to switch majors from medicine to physical education.

Most of those who transfer will earn their degrees.

Perhaps this fact relieves us of some of the concern we might otherwise feel about a transfer student. If he obtains a degree, we tend to think that all else is unimportant. Yet, there is no real difference between the superior student who switches majors, and the one who transfers to another school, and the one who quits college altogether, insofar as each is seeking to assuage his disappointments through a form of escape. Society, however, prefers to take a different view. It would say of the first student that "he has found himself," whether he has or not. Of the second, it says, "he could not get what he wanted at his first college." (He probably did not get it at the second, or the third, but since he wound up with a diploma, we tend to think *that* was what he was seeking.) But when a superior student drops out of college, never to return, both college and society put on sackcloth and ashes, mourning "the loss." Loss to whom? Society thinks the student has lost an opportunity to succeed in life. The college thinks the dropout is a "loss" to the academic community and that he is foolishly excluding himself from a life of the mind. The collegiate view is somewhat presumptuous, for it fondly imagines that the academic community is the only one worth belonging to (but that it needs all the membership it can get), and that a life of the mind is lived best, if not lived only, within the sacred groves. The problem here is that neither college nor society has an Instant Rationalization ready at hand to explain the dropout. Wherefore, both deny him a right to seek happiness in his own way, even if it is necessary to his health and sanity for him to quit college.

151

8

A matter of choice

One fact of American life is that six out of every ten college students discover that the college of their choice is the wrong place for them. They either flunk, transfer, or drop out of it. This has been true for each of the past forty years. Despite changes in the nation's fortunes, despite changes in the colleges, despite the fact that each incoming freshman class has proved brighter than the last, despite increasing social and parental pressure to go to college, the "attrition rate," as the colleges call it, has remained exactly the same. It was, and is, 60 per cent.

Ultimately, 60 per cent of all who enter a college are graduated from somewhere at some time. This means that two of every six dropouts will return to formal education to earn their degrees at the schools they originally entered, or at some other college to which they transferred. But four of every ten students who enter college will drop out, never to return.*

The only new factor in the situation is that the act of leaving has become more painful than it was in 1924, because America has meanwhile bought the idea that everyone who can do college work should go to college. This is a wrong idea, but its prevalence has enriched private psychiatrists. America's belief that a college education is, or should be, the sole passport to success also helps make quitting a traumatic shock both to the dropouts and to their families. Faced with the fact that six of every ten students *do* quit, four of them forever, we are left with several questions to answer. Why do they quit? What should we, their parents, teachers, and society, think of their leaving? What will they do now?

One reason why a great many depart is pathetically simple. They fail.

Most of those who fail do so early on, and most of them fail because they lack the wit and/or a sufficient high school preparation to master the work offered in the college they entered. These involuntary dropouts include the victims of unduly ambitious parents who have pushed, pleaded, or sometimes actually purchased their son's way into a more rigorous college than he should have entered. Here are the victims of those high school principals who, to build a record for placing graduates in college, blandly recommend dull students to deans of admission. Here, also, are the thousands of hapless victims of "selection after admission."

* Statistics reported by U.S. Office of Education, Department of Health, Education and Welfare. Material in this chapter first appeared in *Life* magazine in June, 1963.

The term describes the practice of state universities bound to admit all state residents who meet rudimentary standards set by law. In a few states, a high school diploma is regarded as a sufficient qualification, no matter how poorly the student may have done in the worst of the state's high schools. There is merit in the principle, for it gives everyone an opportunity to enter college; but once having admitted a student, the university is by no means bound to keep him. In the event, more than half the incoming freshmen at such a state university are ruthlessly flunked out within the first term as the university whittles the student body down to a manageable size, selecting those who will actually be able to do the work the university will later demand.

One account, perhaps apocryphal, has it that a railroad serving one Big Ten university town puts on extra cars two weeks after the fall term opens, to haul away the thousands of freshmen who are annually flunked out at that time. What is not apocryphal, but a fact, is that one state university has three admission dates for freshmen. Those who stood in the bottom third of their high school classes are admitted in the summer term; those in the middle third, in the winter term; those in the upper third, in the fall term. The dean of admissions explained that most of those admitted in summer would never see the fall at that university; that a great many of the winter admittees would not be there in the spring, but that most of those students admitted in the fall would survive to be graduated. The university facilities could not possibly accommodate all three groups at once, he said, and the problem seemed to be how to get rid of the greatest number of inept or unprepared students at

154

times most convenient to the university. The summer offered the best occasion, he said, adding that "at any rate, they can all say they've been to college."

The practice of selection after admission is the university's means of defense against unrealistic state legislation; it is the school's compromise with a society that somewhat psychotically demands that every youngster attend college if he possibly can. Yet the practice seems coldly cynical. At best, it is a cruel disappointment to those youngsters who, through no fault of their own, had been told that attending college was an indispensable good on which their futures depended, and so were led or crammed into a situation in which they predictably failed. One might believe they all should have been given the opportunity to try to do college work, but one feels sorry they were so misguided as to have taken advantage of it. Their ephemeral freshman careers are no real service to them, and while on campus they present an unwanted problem to their classmates and to the already overcrowded and harassed universities—a problem which the universities solve summarily enough, but not without a considerable wastage of everyone's time, money, and effort. The flunk-out, dropout rate at nonselective colleges contributes heavily to the national 60 per cent figure; the rate ranges from 20 to 40 per cent at the selective private schools. Here, it might be said that, for the right students—and maybe they amount to 40 per cent of the total—the American college offers a reasonable approach to an education. But it can also be said that for most youngsters college is *not* the right place; certainly most of the failures should never have been admitted.

While failure because of lack of ability or preparation is understandable, it is less easy to understand, or sympathize with, those students who can do the work, but who don't do it, or who decide to stop doing it. One third of those who voluntarily drop out of America's colleges are in good academic standing when they leave. Most intellectually gifted dropouts, however, are failing when they resign.

"Sure, you can say they failed, because they did," one admissions officer said. "But these bright kids *never* fail for academic reasons."

It was his opinion that unresolved emotional problems, such as those suggested in previous chapters, were responsible for every single case of failure at selective colleges, and he cited examples at his own. One boy's problem seemed to be simplicity itself: the girl's father refused to agree to the marriage. The admissions officer said the story went like this:

The girl's father yanked her out of college and packed her off to Switzerland, while the boy drifted heartsick around the campus, letting his hair grow and his work slide because all the meaning of his young life had suddenly been taken away. From here on, the pattern became painfully familiar. The boy's next paper was late. He began to cut classes. The work piled up and he got little done. Stung by the resultant low grades, he told his classmates and himself that "nothing we're asked to study has anything to do with external reality. Look what's happening in the South. So they give us Max Weber and French verbs."

Because he was a gifted student, and because it is never difficult to find something wrong with even the best of colleges, the boy had no trouble creating a towering edifice of sophomoric logic and rationalizations.

156

Philosophy, he said, was ridiculous. For one thing, it was clear there were no final answers to anything, so it was a waste of time to pretend there could be. Plato turned out to be sentimental Fascist; Aristotle was merely a man who gave names to his ignorance; John Stuart Mill was an ass. If you wanted to study mathematics, all you needed was a math book. Sociology was as stupid as it was unreadable, because obviously there could never be such a thing as a science of human society, inasmuch as people are infinitely variable.

Thus he argued, and out he went—resigning at the college's suggestion that he take a year off. Ostensibly, he was an academic failure. In fact, he was a lasslorn Romeo. To say he should have acted otherwise is to say he should have been forty-five instead of nineteen years old.

A good many parents and some college deans would say that boys like Romeo chiefly need a good kick in the slats, but the majority view is to take the dropout's complaints seriously. A Cornell study of dropouts says that each student who leaves has at least two major reasons for doing so, and two minor reasons as well. If most often the "reasons" seem to be the worst kind of juvenile flapdoodle, they are nonetheless overwhelming to the dropout, and sometimes the complaints are quite sound. Robert Iffert says we must discard the notion that all blame should attach to the students, because "this is a two-way operation, and the institutions are also responsible." In a distinct minority was the Cornell boy who icily informed his roommate that "The kid who drops out just can't take it."

"What kind of Rotary Club do you come from, George?" his roommate shot back. "Can't take *what?*

What's this *take* business? Who says you have to take *anything*? I don't mind a guy dropping out as long as there is something positive to be gained, and if the individual is going to take all the responsibility for his actions and has some plans for *not* being in school. Are you saying that duty cannot be shirked? Since when is it a duty to go to college? Everybody's first duty is to realize himself. The pleasure principle says the only reason anyone does anything is for some reward. Suppose the kid realizes that he is not realizing himself and is being pushed into a slot where he doesn't want to go? All right, maybe he doesn't know what's best for himself, but at least he knows this particular slot isn't for him, and he ought to get his head out, before he's pushed all the way in, and look around to see if there isn't a better place for him, somewhere else."

"That's immature," George said. "Everybody has a duty to other people. If a kid is accepted by a college, he has a duty to the college—he is taking up space some other kid could use. He has a duty to his parents, who are forking out the dough."

"Get your head out of it, George," his roommate said. "Aren't parents just trying to create something that pleases them, rather than pleasing the kid? It is not the job of the person who receives a gift to say thank you, it is the job of the person who is giving it to say thank you, because he is having the pleasure of giving the gift. If parents want to give their kids a college education, they should be happy that they can give him one, but if he doesn't want it, they should recognize that this is his decision. Who's going to college, anyway? The parents?"

When a boy holds these views, nothing prevents

158

him from acting on emotion or impulse. Staying in or dropping out is no longer an intellectual decision based on one's view of the worth of academic discipline.

"I want to quit school, but I want to marry a college girl," one University of Pennsylvania student said. "But what college girl is going to want to marry a dropout?"

"Did you ever think that she might marry you because she likes you, and not because you went to college?" a roommate asked.

"Sure, but where do you meet college girls? You meet them in college."

"If you're unhappy, you're unhappy," a Reed boy said. "The fact is that you're unhappy. Sure, there's a reason for it, but it doesn't make you any happier to know why you're unhappy. I mean, you don't have to have a *reason* to get out, when the reason is, you're unhappy."

Sometimes the unhappiness stems from the fact that the dropout had a wonderfully clear idea of what to expect in college but was bitterly disappointed by the reality. In her application for admission, one girl wrote:

"I have always pictured learning as a communication between minds on a Greek hillside in the summer morning, and college seems to offer something like this."

But when she arrived, she found that it rained all the time on those academic uplands. The communication between minds took the form of sitting in conference sessions with bright, aggressive youngsters across the table who would say, "Yeah, but you contradicted yourself by this, this, this, and this," and she had no answer. It was not a conversation on a hillside; it was being pinned to a wall.

In such cases, a pattern often ensues: She looks elsewhere for communication, and finds it in the form of a boy who seems to have problems of his own. And so they are married, and drop out together.

Here, we should note that the national dropout statistics are *not* influenced by girls who "leave college to marry." Proportionately as many women drop out as men, but it is usually more accurate to say "she left college *and* got married," than it is to say, "she left college *to* get married," or "she went to college to *get* married." To be sure, some girls frankly admit they go to college to look for husbands, taking note of the national rumor about the college graduate earning $100,000 more during his lifetime than the high school graduate. It is also true that some girls transfer to look for better husband material than their first school seemed to provide. But in most cases the girl who leaves college and marries is one who does not want to, or cannot, do college work.

Dropping out is sometimes merely a matter of campus geography, as a University of Michigan study suggests. Because of the tremendous social pressure on a student to remain to be graduated, it is not surprising that potential dropouts seek allies. They incessantly talk to their roommates, to anyone who will listen, trying to rally support and convince themselves. In the process, they often convince others. Pockets of discontent appear whenever two or three students in one end of a corridor talk of quitting, and the next thing the college knows, there are empty beds in the dormitory.

"They represent this as a legitimate alternative,

perhaps exotic, sensational, and in many ways attractive to younger and impressionable students, and pretty soon four or five of them have gone their ways," a dean of students complained.

More than 180 studies have been made in an attempt to determine why students leave college, and the gist of them is that no one can predict who will drop out, or say, precisely, why anyone does. The safest generalization is that many students leave for many different reasons, all of which seem good to them if to no one else, and that each dropout must be considered unique, and not lumped into some opprobrious category. The next question is: What *should* we think of our bright youngsters who quit college?

One Philadelphia mother went into nervous collapse when her son walked out of Princeton in his junior year.

"She was just thinking of herself," her son said bitterly.

On hearing this scene described, Robert Iffert sighed.

"I hope we can get some instrumentality of communication that will educate parents and society in general against this notion that if you start to go to college, but don't finish, or even if you don't go to college, you are a misfit in society, or that you have violated some obligation which, of course, is an artificial obligation," Mr. Iffert said. "I don't know what the solution to this problem of stigma, or scar, is."

Writing in *The American College*, Nevitt Sanford says ". . . withdrawal is not . . . a misfortune for the student or for the college every time it happens. Sometimes it is the best way to correct an obvious mistake, or to induce a necessary facing of reality; sometimes students withdraw before graduation because they have already gained from their college all that could be expected. Leaving college, not to enter any other, may leave a student with a sense of unfinished business that will, in some cases, provide motivation for learning for the rest of his life."

Unfortunately, American society shows no indication of taking such a charitable view.

"The way society's set up now," said the headmaster of a preparatory school, "a kid who gets out of the system can only think, 'There's no place for me. I'm not wanted. I'm not needed.'"

Common sense, if not common decency, would suggest that we treat the dropout as an individual, instead of treating him as if he were a madman, a leper, or an unusual statistic. After all, six out of every ten of today's college freshmen will come straggling home sometime between this year and the next, having quit college at least temporarily.

Their parents might well take the view that these are not dropouts, but are their sons and daughters— each in need of food, shelter, and sufficient rest to ease their minds. For the most important thing about a dropout is not that he is no longer in college. It is that he must answer this question: "What am I going to do now?"

Most irritating of the dropouts—to the college authorities—are those the deans call the "womb babies," who cannot leave the vicinity of the campus. They fill the empty spaces in cheap apartments neighboring the city colleges; finding work in nearby bookstores, record shops, and coffee houses; accepting such jobs as that of assistant trainee buyer of men's underwear for a department store; selling Fuller brushes. They are uniformly scornful of the jobs they find, regarding them as an evil necessary to the purchase of paperback books and records, and to paying the rent on the one-room apartment whose chief, if not only, article of furniture is the mattress on the floor. In Cambridge, some melt into what is known as the Harvard Underground—an accumulation of beatniks; of young people who were never admitted to any college but who pretend to be Radcliffe and Harvard students; of dropouts and failures from Boston's several colleges. When they hang around a campus, they attend the lectures, crash the dances, look for dates, and return to the dormitories to talk with former classmates, wearing an aura of furtive bravado not without poignant charm. One boy lived for months on a Western campus, bedding down for the night in a sleeping bag under the bushes bordering the lawn; sleeping in parked cars when it rained; for a while actually living in the dormitories until flushed out by the authorities; supported by a group of students who smuggled him food from the dining hall. He was, an admiring student said, "Kind of far out. But he had more girls than anybody."

"What do you want to call these kids 'womb babies' for?" one student asked. "What's wrong with hanging around? My God—they're *the only real students* at the college. Why shouldn't they go to the lectures? Why shouldn't the lectures be free to anyone who is interested? It shouldn't make any difference to the professor, because he should want to share his learning with people. The college pays him to teach *people*, and he should be glad to talk to an audience that is seriously interested in what he has to say. These kids, as you yourself say, listen to records and read paperbacks. They really want to learn. What they *don't* want to do is waste their time on a lot of junk that somebody thinks they have to have to get a degree. Why sit down and write a paper on somebody's half-witted economics theory when you can spend the same time learning something worth while, talking with some aware guys in the apartment? College isn't, for God's sake, courses and papers—it's the only place where you can meet and talk with aware guys. So the people who hang around, as you say, may be more interested in actually learning something than some of the clods who just sit in classes, taking anything somebody gives them, never questioning anything, just grinding out the old bull to get a degree."

College authorities take a dimmer view of the hangers-on. To them, the womb babies are at best a bother, and at worst a kind of cancer, as one dean put it.

Most dropouts leave the college town to seek their fortunes in the wide world, but they seem to find one another as if drawn by magnets. Whole colonies of them silt up in esoteric little worlds in New York City and San Francisco, where they help to convince themselves it "took real guts" to quit school. Many are found in the North Beach area of San Francisco, living in the narrow, two-family town houses now gone to seed; young people in a low-rent neighborhood, poor, honest, and deadly serious, holding meager jobs and continuing a sort of student life. Indeed, the first characteristic of dropouts—if any generalization can be made—is that they tend to overcompensate, driving hard toward education now that they have left college. The beatnik pad or the Spartan apartment is normally filled with paperback books of irreproachable quality, and the job-holding dropout very often embarks on more intensive reading than regularly enrolled students are required to undertake.

"You hear a lot of stuff about wild parties and beatniks," one young San Franciscan said, "but do you know what a party really is? It's a lot of kids sitting on the floor leaning against the walls, talking. It's subject matter and beer. It's novels and music and poetry and structural analysis and information theory."

If dropouts have anything in common, it is their youth and their need for a program. High school and college offered them a closely structured program, and when they step out of the system, they must have, or invent, some system of their own. Frequently they do have plans, but often the goals are grandiose, and the reality shocking. One young Midwestern couple who dropped out of school together came to North Beach with all sorts of plans. Free from the hampering requirements of courses and term papers, she could now give full time to her poetry; he to the vast and intricate novel of our time that would be based on the structure of Dante's *Inferno*. Believing his work was more demanding than hers, they decided she would support them. Thus, while she worked as a salesgirl, he labored on his novel by a process of minding the baby that had so unexpectedly arrived; by drinking coffee and discussing Zen with the unemployed friends who dropped in during the day seeking enlightenment, and by doing the shopping and the housework. After some months of this, she came home and he went to work, and the poems and the novel have yet to be written.

The not-infrequent end of such a story is that the boy who scornfully accepts the Philistine job of trainee in the underwear department begins to find something to the job, after all. By the end of his first year out of college, he has perhaps received promotion to assistant buyer, and a mercantile future begins to look promising. Or he has taken a job that captured his imagination the minute he heard of it. Only the learned professions are barred to him. He begins to succeed at whatever he does—if he really works at it—because he has the qualities that got him into a selective college in the first place. Most important, he has realized that if he is not writing the novel, it is because he really didn't want to try to write it. So, the world at last brings him face to face with himself, and in the process he may discover the real reasons why he quit college. The process most often takes a year, sometimes longer, but the end of it is predictable; and when his self-doubts are finally resolved, he is truly free to get on with the business of living his life. If he finds that a college degree is indeed essential to promotion in the field he decides upon, the chances are that he will return to college. Two out of every six dropouts do. But if he finds that a degree is *not* essential to success in the field he has entered, and if he is happy and effective in that field, then he will most probably not return to college. Four years later, he will look back on his college leave-taking and wonder what all the shouting had been about. Ten years later, he will have forgotten all about it. Such, at any rate, is the pattern in those cases that have come to the author's attention.

It is true, however, that a great many men will attribute their relative lack of success in their fields to the fact that they dropped out of college, or never went. "If I had only got my degree," they will say, "I'd be further ahead." But it is also the author's belief that the men who say this would have got no further had they received a dozen degrees; that what apparently hinders them in the performance of their jobs has nothing to do with their formal education.

No matter what frame of mind a college dropout may arrive at in future, it is very plain that the moment of his leaving is painful and that he badly needs a suitable program. We have subjected our children to such pressure to make them believe that a diploma is a necessity that leaving college seems to them like the end of the world. They may well suffer the pangs of the suicide who, halfway down the face of the cliff from which he leaped, has suddenly change his mind.

Such was certainly the case with a boy I shall disguise as Tom. You will find the elements of his story familiar. At some risk of redundance, I tell his story here because it seems to encapsulate, in the actual experience of a youngster of our time, the pressures, attitudes, and torments that bear upon a bright lad who, simply because he was highly intelligent, was encouraged—if not commanded—to enter what most of us would regard as the nation's leading university:

His hair was too long. His shirt collar was frayed. There was an empty, haunted look about him. He needed a shave. Two years ago, Tom had come to college all pink-cheeked, crew-cut, and drip-dried, riding an unbroken wave of success. But then the wave broke suddenly on an uncharted reef, and the tide went out.

Now Tom moved vaguely among the four rooms of the double suite, listlessly packing. It was difficult for him to decide in what part of what suitcase to put his soiled clothes; where to put the newly laundered shirts; what to do about his typewriter table. He filled paper cartons with books. Somehow, he couldn't quite get them to fit. At length he piled them in anyhow.

He decided to leave his roommates the rug he had bought. His roommates were in class. In another suite, someone played a recorder.

Tom left off his packing and found an apple in the refrigerator he and his roommates had installed in a closet. He slumped in a corner of the sofa which, lacking one leg, was propped up by bricks. He ate mechanically, in a tired sort of way. He was emotionally exhausted by the struggle that had taken place within himself for the past two years, and he could not really say what had happened to him, or why he had done what he had done. He had tried to put it all into the letter he had written home:

"My decision to leave is based on the conviction that I would be more productive if my work were my own, and thus more meaningful to me," he wrote. "Specifically, what I think is unimportant about college is that exams and courses seem arbitrary, and obviously are compromises. Professors themselves apologize for the fact that they must omit material because of time limitations, and they never agree among themselves on what material should be included. Thus, one professor's reading list for one English course differs wildly from another's for the same course. Exams, which at best ought to provide a student with initiative to organize and learn course material, are superfluous to anyone with a serious interest. . . . So I have decided to take my education into my own hands, in an effort to make my work more meaningful to me by purifying the act of obtaining knowledge and by setting my own goals. . . . The agreement I tacitly made to myself was to find out what I wanted to do, and now that I at least see clearly what I don't want to do, my purpose here is over. I feel free to leave because I think it is the only responsible thing for me to do, and that if I do not leave, I will be setting a precedent for not doing what I should."

One problem with that letter was that Tom did not know whether it was the truth. It had always been important to him to tell the truth, and it had never been so important as it was now. Everything he had said in the letter was true, as far as it went, but was it the *whole* truth?

Despite what he had said about his courses, Tom had no real quarrel with Harvard. For he had also written to his parents that "You can't say Harvard is bad, or that education is a bad thing. Education is a good thing, and in leaving college, I am not leaving education." He went on to say that he had got out of formal education all that it had to offer him personally; that now he had been introduced to the community of great minds, he felt competent to read and study by himself. He put this angrily to a classmate who accused him of being a quitter.

"College separates the men from the boys," Tom said. "The men get out, and the boys stay in."

Partial truths; brave words; angry words. But how much of all this was sheer rationalization to cover some personal failure? Tom suspected there was something badly wrong with him because, being bright enough to get into Harvard, he was also intelligent enough to know why he should not chuck a Harvard education out the window. Yet it was clear to him that he *had* to leave, although he could not say why. He seriously wondered if he was going mad. He considered going to the college psychiatric clinic, but dismissed the idea in disgust. He had been brought up to stand on his own two feet.

"Either you can carry the ball, or you can't carry the ball," he told a roommate who had urged him to talk with either a dean or a psychiatrist. "The real failure is when you chuck the ball to somebody else and say, 'O.K., you carry it for me.' "

Tom was in no academic trouble—at least, not from the college's point of view. But he regarded the straight A's he had won as ridiculous. He attributed his good grades to cheap intellectual trickery on his part and to his instructors' stupidity. To get good grades, you simply spat back what they fed you, and when they heard you repeat what they said, they thought you were brilliant. It was disgusting. Meanwhile, Tom could see no connection between what he was asked to do in class, and anything that made sense to him. The fact that he had found nothing that made sense to him, either in college or in the outside world, deepened his unease. He had sensed from the beginning of his first freshman term that college was no place for him, but he had tried to stick it out, and two years of uncertain drift had changed him from a strong, confident boy into the nervous smoker of too many cigarettes who now sat listless and alone on a broken couch, listening to someone play a recorder in another room, staring at nothing and too tired to concentrate on packing his bags.

The letter he wrote home had precipitated a family crisis. For four generations, each male of his line had gone to Harvard. Not going was unheard of, and *quitting* was unthinkable. A family friend sweetly asked Tom's mother, "I suppose you are asking yourselves where and how you failed as parents?" Tom's father had flown to Boston in a sputtering rage.

"You are a mental and moral coward," he assured his son. "When you accepted a scholarship, you made a contract. Now you are going back on your word just to please yourself."

The idea of leaving Harvard to obtain an education was positively asinine, Tom's father said. Didn't the boy know that Harvard was the greatest university in the world? Where else could a better education be had? Didn't Tom know that being asked to go to Harvard was the greatest compliment a boy could receive? And how did Tom think he was going to get a job without a college diploma?

Tom looked up at his father from weary depths of his own. He had been weighing these, and even better, arguments for staying, against his distaste for formal education. Slowly, he tried once more (as he said) to clue the old man in.

"For the last fifteen years," the boy said, "ever since kindergarten, I've been doing what other people wanted me to do. They said do well in school, so I did well in school. They said be an athlete, so I made the football team. They said be popular, so I was president of the student council. They said do extracurricular things, so I was editor of the magazine. They said go to Harvard, so I went to Harvard. Now, when I want to get out, to do something for myself, they jump all over me."

"All right, what do you want to do?"

"I don't know yet," Tom said slowly. "But whatever it is, it's going to be my idea."

"I suppose you think you're going to sit around here and mope until some bright idea comes to you?" his father asked.

"Yeah," Tom said with cold anger. "I thought I would. The board bill's paid to the end of the term, isn't it?"

171

The boy's father left from Boston airport as angry and as confused as he had come, but not before firing such parting salvoes as, "Don't you realize what you've done?" and "I'll try to find some way to console your mother," which left Tom even deeper in the morass of guilt, shame, and self-doubt than he had been before his father came.

Sitting alone in his Harvard suite, half packed to leave, Tom spoke slowly of his father's visit. He said he had begun to suspect some of the truth about himself.

"Everybody here was somebody," he said. "Everybody else knows why he's here and what he wants to do. I was the guy who wasn't anybody."

He had come to Harvard as the high school whiz, only to find that everybody else had been the high school whiz, too, many of them being far brighter than he. That hurt, he said. It was hard to take. No one applauded him any more. He earned good grades, and still no one cheered. The nagging thing about his grades was that they proved nothing to him, except to confirm him in his knowledge that he was not—by temperament or inclination—a scholar. His studies were preparing him for acceptance in a graduate school of English, and he did not want to go to graduate school, nor, for that matter, did he particularly want to major in English or in any other subject. His position at Harvard seemed to him to be that of a rowboat drifting about in the middle of a yacht race.

"All I know is that it's time for me to do something for myself," he said. "I want to get a part-time job that will give me enough money to rent an apartment but give me enough time to work on projects of my own."

172

Did he have any projects in mind?

"I want to write some plays; get some reading done," he said.

He stared out the window to see the crews practicing on the Charles. There was a clatter of feet on the stone stairs, and the door opened and four boys came in, looking curiously at Tom and his visitor.

"Leaving, Tom?" one of them asked. "You getting out today?"

"Yes," he said.

"You realize you're leaving me with no roommate for next year, don't you?"

Tom smiled. It was not much of a smile. Perhaps it was the smile of a boy who, now that the gloomy, empty suite had become gay, populous, and alive, was remembering all of the good times and none of the bad. For if going to college is like getting married, and leaving it like divorce, there are bad times in the best of marriages and moments of tenderness in the worst. And so the boy who was leaving college to do he knew not really what, other than that it would be something of his own doing, smiled wanly. He reached above the desk he had used and lifted down the book ends that someone had given him as his high school graduation present, when all the world had faith in him.

Tom looked for a long while at the legend on the book ends. At last, speaking very slowly, and so softly that he may have been speaking to himself, he said:

"It's like taking down the Christmas tree."

He put the book ends carefully into a suitcase laid out on the bed he had slept in. He wrapped them carefully in a sweater, and he very carefully and tightly closed the lid and locked the snap and tightened the straps.

173

9

Some reasonable
alternatives

With a crust in his pocket, a merry smile on his frank, open face, and with his father's blessings in his heart, John Youth strode briskly down the highroad to seek his fortune in the wide world.

Three hundred pages later, John would marry the princess and live in the castle, thoughtfully providing his aging parents with a comfortable cottage nearby, where he could visit his mother every day.

Today, the story is a little different. It goes like this:

Because his mother made him do it, John Youth raced out of the house, through high school and straight into a good college and out the other side, into a good safe job. Without pausing for breath, he dashed off to suburbia with a nice, safe wife who promptly produced three quick children, who began running, too.

Something has happened between Then and Now,

174

which is a pity, for the nature of Youth has not essentially changed. Youngsters still want to see the world. They want to explore on their own; to sniff at the bones of experience like apprehensive but fascinated puppies. They like to fiddle around to no apparent purpose, doing little that seems to make much sense. They have no idea of time, but a great trust in the distant future. Meanwhile, they want the right to make their own mistakes.

The significant change seems to be that we, Youth's elders, have come charging into the scene, urging speed. We want our children to stop wasting time. We hurry them toward adult life, towing them every step of the way, indulging them to the point where they have no opportunity to develop their personalities or sense of responsibility, pressing adult concepts and adult toys upon them as gifts, and demanding that they immediately use them. But young people are not in all this hurry. A good many of them are properly suspicious of it and are by no means sure that we are taking them in a direction they want to go. More than a few want to grow up in their own way, on their own time.

Of course there are exceptions to this pattern, but the over-all impression is that we do not seem to care enough for our children to have the simple decency to let them be themselves. Consider the different views of Steve and his father:

"If Steve doesn't go to college, he will never be able to join the club, and if he doesn't join the club, he will never make any money," the boy's father said. "It's as simple as that, and if he can't see it, he is a damned fool."

"Man," Steve said, "if my Pop wants me to go to college just so I can make a crock of dough and wind up in that goofy club with those other yuks, he is One, Two, Three, O-U-T."

Steve is not thinking of a distant future. It so happens that he intends to go to college, not because he envisions a career, but because all his friends are going, and he wants to live a life of his own, now, with his contemporaries. This is a perfectly legitimate reason for wanting to attend college, and it makes much more sense than his father's reason. It speaks directly to the central, unique value of the collegiate experience.

"The people you meet in college offer you far more of an education than the professors you meet or the courses you take," a Reed senior said.

"You know why the Ivy schools are better than this place?" a Temple sophomore said. "It's because the kids who go there are brighter than we are."

All three youngsters are echoing the thoughts of observers as different as Cardinal Newman and Stephen Leacock: College is the people who attend it.

The Cardinal said that if he had to choose between living in a dormitory or attending classes as a means of acquiring an education, he would choose the dormitory. Mr. Leacock said if he were to found a university, he would first found a smoking room. As funds became available, he said, he would add a library, a dining hall, a dormitory. Were any funds remaining, he might consider hiring a professor.

The view here is that a college is valuable insofar as it resembles a conversation among bright people. Perhaps a father of three sons might believe that $36,000 is a relatively large amount of money to pay for their enjoying four years of chitter-chatter in Princeton's comfortable suites, but he should know that the informal education that begins when classes end is the heart and soul of a college education.

"I know this brilliant atheist," a Catholic student at a city university said. "If you want to know, he's actually my best friend. He's my roommate. It's not that I'm losing my faith, or anything like that. It's just that I never really thought about it before I had to defend it."

"I'd never read anything past *Ivanhoe* in high school," said a boy at a Midwestern university. "But when I came here, I found all these kids from New York talking about guys you never heard of, like Camus and Dostoevsky. It was amazing. I didn't know what they were talking about, but I found out in a hurry. It was either that, or I'd have been out of it."

The Midwestern boy's reasons for wanting to read Camus might seem callow, but the net result could not be called harmful. Many a professor would say that the particular virtue of college lies in the fact that it is the only social institution we have wherein a man may dwell for a time surrounded by a disproportionate number of bright people, against whose wits he hones his; wherein every intellectual facility is provided him; where he is under no obligation other than to speculate as widely and as deeply as he wishes over libraries of information set before him.

The most poignant lessons would seem to be those one learns in youth from one's contemporaries, and at college these are learned in the dining halls, in intellectual argument in a dormitory room, in all the places young men and women meet on and around the campus; in the simple stuff of living in enforced intimacy with a few hundred total strangers. The special quality of these encounters is that they all—

177

even the girl's date in the boy's room—are somehow connected with some degree of concern for affairs of the mind. In no other social institution save primary and secondary school is the ordinary life of the institution concerned with anything of the sort.

How much any student profits from free-form discourse is, of course, up to him. Some will find it boring and pointless. Everything would seem to depend upon the individual student's personality and fund of information. (One Harvard boy took the lofty view that it would waste his time to talk with his freshmen roommates because they did not know enough to be able to speak with him. Their view of him was that his personality was not impressively engaging.) There is no way to measure how much a student will learn from his friends during his college years, and much less can we evaluate the quality of whatever he might have learned. Nor can anyone say how long a student must stay on any particular campus in order to glean all he can from his contemporaries. There is no particular reason to believe the process must take four years. Generally speaking, those who derive most from their collegiate experience are bright youngsters of gregarious nature who were never challenged in mediocre high schools and who come from minimal cultural backgrounds. Those who profit least are well-traveled youngsters who come from intellectual homes and who have attended superior public or private schools. Briefly, the first group learns more things worth learning from the second group than the second group learns from the first. In any event, it is difficult to say that, apart from bringing people together for the purposes of intellectual discourse, a college does anything else that is uniquely valuable.

To be sure, a college provides courses of instruction. But so does a night school. It has a library. But so does any major city. It provides an opportunity for people to learn to live together. So does a rooming-house. It gives youngsters an opportunity to look after themselves. But so does a hobo jungle. College may indeed be a place offering the most convenient and maximum opportunities in all these regards, but it is not the only place in which life's basic lessons may be learned or information acquired. It is unique only in its aspect as a contentious forum.

Not all adolescents are going to profit uniformly, from either the formal or the informal education a college can provide. In fact, not all adolescents should attend, and not all of them do. For that matter, there is not the slightest reason, except social convenience, why our colleges concern themselves exclusively with adolescents in the first place. Indeed, there is reason to believe they should not, for as one professor put it (paraphrasing Shaw), "It is a pity that education is wasted on the young."

He was not being flippant, for he went on to say that a man needs some experience in the outside world in order to bring value to the campus; in order to appreciate the insights that the academic world can provide. Proof, he said, lies in the splendid college records made by returned veterans of the Second World War, and in the academic records of industrial executives who attend special humanities programs sponsored at certain colleges by business corporations.

The professor therefore suggested that college should not necessarily be what happens immediately after high school, but that it should be something a growing man can enter, leave, and return to at need at any time of his life. His view embraced the fact that learning—formal and informal—proceeds in fits and starts throughout life, and that all institutions of learning should accommodate themselves to this fact.

Drastic changes would take place in the collegiate world if this line of thinking were pursued, and it is easy to predict that it will be pursued, because the circumstances of national life favor it. As society becomes increasingly affluent and increasingly freed by machines from humdrum chores, there is more time and money to spend on the pleasures of life, which of course include education. We are now seeing a steady increase in the number of housewives who enroll in college once their children are in school. Shorter work hours have increased enrollments in night schools and extension courses. Earlier retirement has made it possible for men in their fifties to embark on college studies preparatory to second careers. There is growing demand for colleges to keep their doors open night and day, all year round. Also part of current thinking is the notion that admission to college might be based on factors other than—and not necessarily including—academic performance in high school. Changes in admission policies would open the doors not only to those who bloomed late, but also to those who for one reason and another did not finish high school, but who during the course of their lives developed aptitude, ability, and need for formal education.

Another suggestion recently heard is that colleges grant credentials other than diplomas and degrees, such as certificates of achievement in subject matter. One professor said this "would shunt out of general education all those whose interests are specific, so that they could go directly to what they wanted at no waste of their time, or of ours." Another professor said he thought the college "should make it possible for an incoming student to first gorge himself on the subject matter he wants, instead of demanding that he first take a lot of subjects he doesn't want, and which often serve to drive him out of education instead of into it."

Their suggestions imply that a college should offer three separate programs. It could reserve its diploma for those students who satisfy the college's scholarly requirements. It could grant a special student a certificate of competence to show a prospective employer. It could offer a different document (since the world seems to cherish documents) to the adolescents who come to college with no well-formed objectives, and who at this moment in their lives might profit more from general survey courses than from deep courses designed as prerequisites to graduate studies.

If a college were to offer these three programs, it would seem wise to keep the lines open among them, so that a student could move without prejudice from one to another as his objectives crystallized in his mind. In any event, current thought tends to regard a student as someone who wishes to study something, and it urges the colleges to accept a candidate at whatever age the student happens to be when he realizes that serious work in the field, at college, will best serve his need.

Rising resentment against the doctrine of publish or perish suggests that the future college will place a premium on good teaching; that teachers will be hired because of their competence in their fields and their ability to communicate what they know, without respect to their formal education. An increasing number of universities now go into the world to find men who have demonstrated their competence. They are hiring unlettered artists, writers, musicians, and dramatists of considerable celebrity. Some of these people are no better able to teach what they know than are some professors, but at least their honors have been won in a more general competition than the academic, and this very fact evokes a certain excitement among the students.

The total shape of current thought and practice suggests that the campus of tomorrow will no longer be almost exclusively populated by late adolescents, but by a student body that contains a more normal balance of young and old, which has a greater concern for realistic study, and which, out of the experience of its members, will provide a far more valuable informal discussion group than any student body of adolescents could. One can only say, Speed the day! for to keep the college doors open at all times to all ages would not only be a service to the general cause of education, but it would almost certainly put an end to the current hysterical insistence that a high school student forfeits all chance of success if he does not win college admission immediately upon high school graduation.

In predicting the shape of future colleges, I am not making original suggestions, but am merely reporting what is now going on. Education, always in flux, is peculiarly sensitive to public mood, despite its apparent remoteness in an ivory tower. It is after all a process of society, and because a good many of the most alert minds in a society will be found in its colleges, changes in the order of things are normally first suggested by the academic community. But changes are almost never effected until the public welcomes them. Moreover, like any other establishment, the academic establishment has a vested interest in remaining exactly as it is. So changes will most probably be made with glacial speed. Yet, ten years from now, the American college will most probably more resemble a community of freely met scholars than it does today. The question is, How much more?

In good part, the answer will depend upon public acceptance of these facts:

Valuable as the collegiate experience can be, it is not always valuable to everyone; no particular magic is worked within an arbitrary four-year period; possession of a diploma is not always a guarantee of anything much; the time for a man to go to college does not necessarily occur during his adolescence; lack of a diploma does not always condemn a lad to limbo; reasonable alternatives to the collegiate experience exist.

By and large, the public mood is such as to allow it to accept these statements as being true, but whether the general public is willing to act on the basis of facts is quite another matter.

Meanwhile, there is much we can do to reduce the crushing weight of anxiety that now bears upon our high school students and their parents. We can begin by remembering how very young the eighteen-year-old is; by realizing how much he may need time to loaf, or hack around, as he calls it. During his apparent aimlessness, he is trying to sort things out. Everyone needs a time for reflection at different stages of his life, and the first stage is set at the moment of high school graduation. The eighteen-year-old is eager to somehow prove himself, but is a bit dubious as to how and where to begin. It is a rare child who flies arrow-straight from home and school directly into his adult career. Most of us—particularly most adolescents —proceed through life more like a blind man making his way up a boulder-strewn hillside. The first job is almost never the last one, nor is the second, nor the third. We live and, as someone hopefully said, learn. The years eighteen to twenty-two are only four out of the seventy, and they are not necessarily the most formative. College authorities assure us that too many students come to college too soon; that the students who will get most out of college, and who are most likely to remain to be graduated, are those who know precisely what they expect the college to do for them. Their deans' thought is that a youngster who spends a year or two in the outside world before coming to college will discover for himself whether possession of a college degree is essential to realization of his developing ambitions.

"The boy of eighteen who is not ready to go to college *can* spend two years that he will later view as respectably spent, and positively spent, and start college at twenty," the dean of admissions at one selective college said. "If it were socially acceptable for a boy to go to work after high school, then two years later he would not suffer the kind of community pressure and high school pressure that comes from being rejected from college today, or not being good enough to get in, or not going where his parents went. By the time he was twenty, he would either be established in a job which both he and the community find acceptable, or he would now be ready to apply for college admission if he found reasons why he should, but, in any event, he would no longer be as much in the public eye as the graduating high school senior, and the pressure would be off."

It should not greatly concern us whether a high school senior goes to college, or whether he signs on a commercial fishing boat, or becomes a ranch hand, or migrant laborer, or quits college to go to sea (as Dana did), or joins the Air Force, or apprentices himself to a trade, or takes a job as a bread truck driver, or just plain hits the road for a year or so of aimless wandering. By the time he is eighteen, and presuming that we have raised him to be a responsible, self-reliant lad, we might as well give him a chance to shift for himself a bit. Indeed, by the time he is eighteen we have otherwise done all we can for him except wave good-bye to him and wish him well, advising him that we will always be glad to see him if he wants to drop by from time to time, and that we will always be glad to be of what help we can if he thinks he needs any help. It is well to remember that what he does at this moment is not necessarily what he will do for the rest of his life; that if he has the good qualities we hope he has, he will eventually find his place in this world. Many alternatives to going to college exist, and not all of them are bad. One of the more worth while is travel abroad.

"I know just big bunches of kids who would get a whole lot more out of a trip to Europe," one college senior said. "And their fathers could send them to Europe for four years for about half as much money as they're paying to send them here."

What would they do in Europe?

"Look at it! Live in it!" the boy said. "Sure, they ought to have some reason to want to go, some idea of what they want to look at. It's the same thing as

185

going to college, you get more out of it if you know what you're doing. But you can't stay there without getting *something* out of it, even just sitting at a cafe having a beer, because it's different.

"Unless," he qualified his statement, "you're just a clod anyway, and if you're a clod you're going to be a clod anywhere. But you take a bright kid who doesn't like college and wants to do something, he's going to flip when he sees Europe. The scales will fall from his eyes. What are we after, anyway? A degree? No. What we're all after is *education,* which is really growing older and having experiences, and meeting other people and getting perspective. Europe is a great place for it— and a lot cheaper than college."

Some parents might object that "going to Europe" sounds like a fairly complicated way of wasting time and money unless there was some specific end in view, but before they speed to that conclusion, they might wish to ask themselves just how *they* spent the past year.

Another perfectly reasonable alternative to college-after-high school is Army enlistment. A rational stranger from another planet might presume that a nation as warlike as ours would hold the soldier in good repute, and expect us to at least understand that bearing arms is one responsibility of male citizenship. No doubt he would be astonished to learn that we look down on the soldier; think the service a waste of time; and that many of our employers view the Army as a place where a man is taught to shirk and loaf.

Actually, the Army is just another social institution that—like college, a business firm, or any other large organization of people—offers loafers and shirkers an opportunity to demonstrate their poor qualities in

186

public. It offers other people infinite opportunities to become what they wish to become. It provides all sorts of vocational training, including work that challenges gifted minds. Army instruction is much more indoctrination than it is education, but many able youngsters are happier with it than they were, or would be, in the free-form college seminar, and they are just as liable to be happier within military discipline than within an unstructured campus or civil life. As one student in an Army school said:

"The Army doesn't horse around. They tell you the deal, you learn it, and that's that."

It is simply not true that Army vocational skills cannot be applied to civilian tasks, as some employers believe. That belief is just as far from reality as the popular belief that all a man does in the service is peel potatoes. If, in fact, all a particular man does in the Army is peel potatoes, the reason for this will be that he is a potato peeler. He would be a potato peeler in civil life, too. The Army is a nation within a nation, self-sufficient and viable. It operates a college, offers college extension courses of all kinds, speaks foreign languages, maintains complicated electronic equipment and power plants, builds every sort of structure, makes roads, drives machines, dredges harbors, fights enemies and—peels potatoes. It works at every kind of profession and trade that one may find in civil life, and perhaps as the civilian world does not, the Army understands that all jobs are necessary and, in that sense, important.

The military service also does something that we might not presume it does. Like college, like any other social institution of some size, it offers an uncertain young man ample opportunity to discover who he is, with respect to a wide cross section of his contemporaries. Its very rigidity encourages self-reliance and inculcates a sense of personal responsibility in those who are most oppressed by paternalistic discipline, because it forces them to seek ways of establishing their personal identity and difference from the ordered ranks.

So the Army serves as haven for those who need to be told what to do, and it serves as a forcing ground of personal decision for those who do not want to be told what to do but who have some difficulty deciding just what it is that they *do* want to do. Meantime, military service offers unparalleled vocational and educational opportunity to any person ready to take advantage of it. It can be a worthy and reasonable alternative to a college education for many a man; perhaps one that imparts certain lessons he would never learn on campus. The most valuable military training programs are not open to short-term draftees, however, but are reserved for high school graduates who volunter for three- and four-year tours of duty. To youth, four years seems an eternity, but the fact is that nowhere else in our society can a young man receive the dollar equivalent in food, clothing, housing, medical and dental care, recreation facilities, job training, foreign travel, paid vacations, and monthly pay, in the four years immediately following high school.

Another reasonable alternative to college attendance, insofar as the narrow acquisition of a vocational skill is concerned, is apprentice training. There are many apprenticeship programs in our industries; many companies send their employees to training schools and colleges, claiming these programs to be legitimate tax deductions. All such activities should be widely extended, but there are two difficulties. One is that it is difficult to convince parents that, since their child is not college caliber, they should abandon their wistful dream that he is, and so save him a wasted trip to the state university that will predictably toss him back. Second, it is not easy to get it through the status-conscious head of the businessman that he should hire people instead of pieces of paper. He must be brought to see that it is more sensible to hire on the basis of job aptitude and personality than on the basis of possession of a diploma and be made to understand that the companies most successful in the retention of employees are those that provide the hired hands with the greatest possibilities of advancement through company-sponsored educational programs. The businessman probably knows that most jobs are best learned on the job, but it is surely difficult to get him to practice whatever he preaches. Perhaps Mr. Iffert might be able to convince him:

"There are many students who have the job skills of a high school level who go to college now, but who do not, while there, increase in their employable skills," Mr. Iffert said. "Now, because they have gone to college, they think they cannot have jobs demanding only high school job skills, and they are therefore unhappy and unsuccessful if they try a job demanding higher job skills, or they are miserable in taking a job they have been led to believe lies at lower-than-college levels. We must get away from the idea that just because you have a degree, you are automatically qualified for a job that demands skills which you may not have acquired during your college years, and from the idea that just because you do not have a degree, you therefore lack college skills you may have acquired somewhere else."

189

In short, if an employer demands specific skills or knowledge, and certain traits of character and personality, he should not care where the applicant acquired them.

The important question posed by a high school graduate is really not where, or whether, he is going to college. It is: What is he going to do now? A wise parent would point out sundry possibilities, including college only if the student had academic abilities, aptitudes, and a desire to use them on college work— but leaving the answer much more up to the student than is now the case. Our only entirely legitimate demand is that he do something. We can hope that what he does will prove wise, but we would be foolish to imagine that such proof will be forthcoming by return mail.

One thing is quite certain: We have been leading our children's lives for them to such an extent that their idea of the importance of winning college admission has become as psychotic as our own. Heretical as it may now seem, candor demands that we should acquaint ourselves and our children with the fact that going to college is not the only path to a useful, happy life. Using the youngsters' own language, we might tell them this:

"College isn't all *that* great. It's great, yes, but not too great. It is mainly just teachers who think college is red, white and blue, *five* trading stamps, and a partridge in a pear tree. Actually, there are about fifty other ways to make the scene, if you want to think about them. But you know something? It takes talent and guts to make the scene in a really great way. If you don't have them, you'll never make it big no matter *how* many colleges you go to. If you do have them, then you'll make it whether you go to college or not."

190